A GREAT MAN OF SCIENCE

An Appraisal of the Works of Fred Hoyle

FRANCIS A. ANDREW

Order this book online at www.trafford.com
or email orders@trafford.com

Most Trafford titles are also available at major online book retailers.

Print information available on the last page.

ISBN: 978-1-4907-5164-1 (sc)
ISBN: 978-1-4907-5165-8 (hc)
ISBN: 978-1-4907-5180-1 (e)

Library of Congress Control Number: 2014921342

Trafford rev. 01/08/2016

www.trafford.com

North America & international
toll-free: 1 888 232 4444 (USA & Canada)
fax: 812 355 4082

Introdcution

One may well ask as to what constituted the motivating drive for me in reading and reviewing all of the works of the late Fred Hoyle. There can be little doubt that Fred Hoyle was one of the 20th century's greatest of men; he was to astronomy what Charles Darwin was to Biology and what Albert Einstein was to Physics. On a more personal note, Fred Hoyle, along with Sir Patrick Moore and Professor N. Chandra Wickramasinghe, were the main inspirational figures in the development of my enthusiasm for the astronomical sciences.

Born in Bingley in Yorkshire in 1915, Hoyle was a controversial individual from his earliest years. His truanting from school to explore the real world around him, helped instill in his character a practical outlook on life and a reputation for bluntness in his diction – Hoyle called a spade a spade!

In the scientific arena, his persistent adherence to the Steady State Theory of cosmic origins distinguished him from most of the astronomical community which accepted the Big Bang orthodoxy in explaining creation. Along with his colleague, Professor N. Chandra Wickramasinghe, Hoyle challenged the conventionalities of the biological and medical sciences by developing the theory of panspermia through which he argued that many of our common diseases have an extra-terrestrial origin and that evolution is a cosmic-wide rather than a merely terrestrial phenomenon. Though many of his critics accused him of devising hypotheses on the flimsiest of evidence, it must be said in defence of Hoyle that he never courted controversy for the sake of controversy; rather it was his openness of mind and broadness of thinking that led him, with the mass of evidence he had accumulated over many years of painstaking research, into the realms of the maverick.

Since Fred Hoyle's death in 2001, his unconventional scientific theories live on. And so it is that this book has been timed to coincide with the 100th anniversary of his birth and to provide a testimony to the fact that his scientific legacy is very much the science of the future.

This book is divided into four sections. Part 1 deals with the biographical and autobiographical works related to Sir Fred Hoyle. Part II consists of the reviews of his scientific works, while Part III concentrates upon works which have an introduction composed by him. Part IV is dedicated to reviews of his science fiction novels, many of which were co-authored with his highly literary talented son, Mr. Geoffrey Hoyle. The views which I have expressed in these reviews are, however, entirely my own.

Acknowledgements

I would like to thank my sister, Mrs. Josephine Burgass, who, by her painstaking searches of antiquarian booksellers, procured for me many of the works of Fred Hoyle. Without her co-operation, I could never have written this book from my current abode in far-off Nizwa, Oman.

Dedication

This book is dedicated to Geoffrey Hoyle, son of the late Fred Hoyle. The works of science fiction that Mr. Hoyle co-authored with his father, did so much to develop my own methodology and skill (such as they are!) as a science fiction writer. Without having read these fascinating novels by the Hoyles, it is doubtful that I would have found the inspiration to compose my own novels from any other source.

PART I

Biographical and Autobiographical

Contents

I) The Small World of Fred Hoyle: *by Fred Hoyle* 5
II) Home is Where the Wind Blows: *by Fred Hoyle* 7
III) A Life in Science: *by Simon Mitton* 9
IV) A Journey with Fred Hoyle: *by Chandra Wickramasinghe* 11
V) The Scientific Legacy of Fred Hoyle: *Sargent, L.W. W. et al.* 13
VI) Fred Hoyle's Universe: *by Jane Gregory* 15

I

The Small World of Fred Hoyle:

by Fred Hoyle

Fred Hoyle opens his first chapter with a discussion of trilby hats. The effect of the trilby hat was that it made the face and head of its wearer appear larger than it actually was. We can only really be cognizant of this fact when we examine it from a historical rather than from a contemporary perspective for facts such as these are best understood within the context of a comparative analysis of the fashions and designs of different eras. This apparent triviality of trilby hats transparently demonstrates the great extent of Hoyle's observational and analytical abilities which, though mainly exercised in scientific fields, could switch to other disciplines and there offer insights of near unfathomable depths such as to shame their practitioners engaged in their full-time study.

In later life, Hoyle bemoaned what he saw as the late 20th century's lack of scientific progress and dearth of scientific ideas all of which stood in stark contrast to the prolific output of scientists in the 19th century and the early part of the 20th century. Hoyle put all this down to science becoming big, corporatist and above all conformist. The straitjacket in which scientists now find themselves confined militates against any originality of thought and development of ideas. That Hoyle always desisted from taking the eggs from birds' nests that he and his friends found, preferring instead to leave them and watch what eventually happened, is not only indicative of his scientifically enquiring mind forming at an early age but of the non-conformity for which he was known throughout his adult life. Hoyle's persistent truancy during the early years of his schooling, his feelings that most of what was given to children to learn was essentially useless, are other examples of the ingredients that went into the making of Hoyle's non-conformity with establishment norms and practices.

The mysterious untimely deaths on the local Milnerfield estate, the dark strip of woodland enclosed by the "Great Wall of Milnerfield" and the eerie Sparrow Bills Lane with its strange twists and turns all of which went into creating a world of ghosts and ghouls and dragons and ogres must have been for Hoyle an imaginative wonderland whose seeds would eventually sprout in his science fiction novels whose characters, plots and themes became almost as well-known as his work as a serious scientist.

"The Small World of Fred Hoyle" has something big to tell us who are living in the opening years of the 21st century. Our world is bigger, but yet it is smaller! We can travel further and faster but we see less. Hoyle's learning about factory machines and canal lock gates were the fruits of a real education whichironically came from his periods of truancy, from the freeing of himself from the confines of the four walls of a brick and mortar classroom. Situations of scarcity of resources which were manifested in an ill-equipped school chemistry laboratory served to throw the pupils back on their own resources and inventiveness. The mythical creatures of Milnerfield and the machinery of the mills were the contrasting blends which made Hoyle at once the practical scientist and the man of fresh ideas and healthy imagination. Is it not astonishing that factories and fairies' dens were the properties of the Salt family of Milnerfield? Do we not see in these starkly contrasting worlds a microcosm of Britain, a nation which has prospered and succeeded on a marriage of tradition and progress, a Britain which Hoyle loved and to which he showed the greatest patriotism.?

In our world of plenty and privilege, inventiveness isa somewhat scare commodity; in a childhood of electronic games and play stations imagination is stunted and the ghosts and ghouls have fled the tree-shaded winding lanes to become mere blips on a computer monitor. Yet, if we re-read the autobiographical works of the late Fred Hoyle and take as our own his commiserations for a long lost past we may have the chance of re-creating the immensity of his small world and in so doing create a bigger and better world of our own.

II

Home is Where the Wind Blows:

by Fred Hoyle

I have always admired Fred Hoyle's works and writings. His autobiography "Home is where the wind blows" is truly Hoyle's masterpiece among all his works. Although the greatest cosmologist of the 20th century, Hoyle remains totally unpretentious throughout this book;whether as a grammar school pupil or Plumian Professor of Cosmology, Hoyle is never far from the earthy rough and tumble Bingley boy of the early years of the last century.

I have been reading Hoyle's works since I was at school, so much of my thinking on science in general and astronomy in particular has been guided by Hoyle's thoughts and ideologies. And yet it is not only in the field of science that Fred Hoyle had much to say throughout his life, he also showed great astuteness in his analyses of matters political. And so it is here that I would make a mild criticism of his autobiography: Hoyle makes only passing reference to his excellent book "A Decade of Decision" and fails to even mention "Man and Materialism" and "Of Men and Galaxies". These earlier works of Hoyle's demonstrate his penetrating insight into political, social and economic issues which were not only germane and central at the time of their composition, but which can be found as being equally relevant in the 21st century. For example in "A Decade of Decision", written in 1950, Hoyle states that there is very little difference between the Conservative and Labour Parties - a fact that is only beginning to dawn on people now. In these early writings, Fred discusses the problem of the exhaustion of fossil fuels and other finite resources, and argues that the best alternative is nuclear energy: and all this being two decades before the oil crisis of 1973.

In "Of Men and Galaxies", Hoyle rightly bemoans the fact that science has produced nothing outstanding since the early decades of the

20th century, and this is because we rely too much on "big science" with the result that scientists cannot think outside of a fixed establishment mind-set. As large funding is necessary for today's science, the scientist has to spend as much time lobbying government for money as in doing actual scientific research. If this were the case in 1964, it must be even more so in 2004.

So this is why I would classify Fred Hoyle as one of the last of the great thinkers and classical scientists of the 20th century. He said what was on his mind and he said it in no uncertain terms. Hoyle was anti-establishment all his life. Today's scientists simply fit into the establishment mold, and that is why the chances of science throwing up another Hoyle are highly unlikely. Like history, science today has its "givens", which, like articles of faith must never be challenged; two of the most prominent of these are evolution and big bang cosmology - but challenge them Hoyle did with his theory of Panspermia and his Steady State concept of the Universe respectively. Today's stock of scientists are merely functionaries with virtually no imagination or originality of thinking. To be fair, perhaps the only exception to this would be the current Astronomer Royal, Lord Rees. Others of Hoyle's generation, now deceased, that ought to be paid tribute to, and who were at some time or another colleagues of Hoyle are Sir Herman Bondi, Thomas Gold, Sir Bernard Lovell and the late Prof. Raymond A. Lyttleton.

III

A Life in Science:

by Simon Mitton

Dr. Simon Mitton has written an excellent biography on the life of the late Fred Hoyle. For those who are interested in the way the science of astronomy has evolved throughout the 20th century and Fred Hoyle's magnificent contribution to its evolution and development, then this is a must-read book.

The Prologue by Paul Davies and the Forward by the author serve to show the context within which Hoyle conducted his career as a cosmologist - the need to put British astronomy back on the map. Throughout the war and during the post-war years, America was far ahead of any other country in the science of astronomy; Hoyle changed all that and made Cambridge a magnet for budding astronomers from all over the world including the United States. That Simon Mitton starts off the first of the twelve chapters into which his book is divided with Hoyle's resignation in 1972 from the Institute of Astronomy in Cambridge would seem to highlight this point. Later in the chapter Dr. Mitton follows the regular pattern of most biographers by treating on the birth and formative years of the young Fred Hoyle.

In a superbly interesting and readable style, Dr. Mitton takes the reader through the years of Hoyle's undergraduate life as a student in Cambridge where he encountered some of the great names of the time in science - most notably Sir Arthur Eddington and Paul Dirac. It was during his graduate years in Cambridge that Hoyle decided that his career lay in astronomy. During the war years, when Hoyle worked on Radar development at the Admiralty, he continued to develop his interests in astronomy in close co-operation with Raymond A. Lyttleton, Herman Bondi and Thomas Gold. It was with Bondi and Gold that Hoyle in the post war years set forth the concept of a steady state Universe and continuous creation; this challenged the prevailing super-dense model (the Big Bang) as an explanation for the origin of the Universe. Dr. Mitton goes on to explain Hoyle's pioneering work in showing how chemical elements are synthesised in the interior of stars.

It could be argued that Simon Mitton has given too much space to the cut and thrust politics involved in astronomy in the UK. This I do not believe is a valid criticism as the problems of bureaucracy and politics in science were among Hoyle's greatest bugbears. In his book "Of Men and Galaxies" Hoyle bemoaned the fact that scientists were spending too much time on non-scientific matters to the detriment of genuine scientific research and innovation. Hoyle was always the unconventional, always the anti-establishment figure, yet the rebel in him consistently veered towards the positive, never the negative. His boyhood truancy from school resulted in his learning much in the area of fluid mechanics by his observation of the operation of the locks on the Leeds-Liverpool canal.

Throughout his life, Hoyle showed a tremendous capacity for hard and productive work; he was a prolific writer not only of scientific fact but of science fiction ("The Black Cloud" and "A for Andromeda") and politics ("Man and Materialism" and "A Decade of Decision")

Hoyle often ventured into areas outside of his own discipline of cosmology and wrote on biology, paleontology and archeology. He is on record as saying that nature does not respect the distinctions between the sciences that academe makes. This principle may well be extended to all the academic disciplines. In his radio talks "The Nature of the Universe", Hoyle quoted Ray Lyttleton as saying that the human brain may be patterned on the Universe. Lyttleton cuts a rather sad figure in Dr. Mitton's book, yet if we consider what a profound and far-reaching statement Lyttleton had made and placed it alongside Hoyle's thesis on linkages between the various scientific and academic disciplinesoverall, then we must ask whether or not there is some connection between neurology and cosmology! Is there thus a blurring in the distinction between the subjective and the objective? Thanks to Hoyle, Lyttleton may be in for some posthumous fame.!

Simon Mitton's biography is a twin volume to Fred's autobiography "Home Is Where The Wind Blows". Hoyle was a man of humility and so his scientific brilliance is very much down-played in "Home", but Dr. Mitton truly brings out in his biography the full genius of Fred Hoyle.

IV

A Journey with Fred Hoyle:

by Chandra Wickramasinghe

In the prologue to "A Journey with Fred Hoyle" Professor Chandra Wickramasinghe states that after Hoyle's publication of his second autobiography "Home is Where the Wind Blows", Hoyle had advised him 'I have made only a passing reference to our long collaboration, because it seemed disconnected from the thesis I was developing there. Ours is an even bigger story that is certainly worth telling. Perhaps you would like to do that one day?'

In the various biographies and autobiographies of Fred Hoyle, hardly any mention is made of the highly controversial theories developed by Hoyle and Wickramasinghe regarding the cosmic origins of life. "A Journey with Fred Hoyle" is therefore the "missing link" in the Hoyle biographical data.

Wickramasinghe begins his book with a background outline of his formative years in Sri Lanka and how he first met Hoyle in Cambridge in 1960. Wickramasinghe discussed with Hoyle the problem with the theory of interstellar grains being composed of ice. Considering the difficulties involved in the formation of water droplets in the terrestrial atmosphere, how much more so then in the lesser densities of interstellar clouds where the numbers of atoms range from only 10 to 100 per cubic centimeter. How then to solve the nucleation problem in interstellar grains?

The rest of this book is an exciting story of how Hoyle and Wickramasinghe, after carefully considering many conventional models regarding the nature of interstellar dust, came to the conclusion that it was in fact desiccated bacteria. Spectroscopic analyses of the dust seemed to confirm the bacterial hypothesis.

After being convinced of the veracity of the bacterial model as an explanation of the nature and composition of interstellar dust, the theory had knock-on effects in other scientific fields. Hoyle and Wickramasinghe developed the hypothesis that bacteria and viruses constantly enter the Earth's atmosphere and are the major causes of diseases such as the common cold and influenza. Their studies of the historic patterns of the spread of influenza epidemics, convinced them that the older theory of person-to-person contact serving as a vehicle for the spread of these diseases was woefully lacking in evidence. Incoming pathogens falling through the atmosphere and being conveyed by wind and rain droplets appeared to fit the bill more accurately.

The alternative model for interstellar grains also impacted on evolutionary theory by challenging the standard Darwinian explanation which accounted for species evolving by gradual adaptation involving minor changes over long periods of time. As the fossil record has consistently failed to support this form of evolution, Hoyle and Wickramasinghe offered an alternative theory which explains evolution as a cosmic rather than a terrestrial phenomenon. The concept of evolution by the adoption of beneficial viruses and bacteria by species was proposed by the two scientists as a more satisfactory way of accounting for the fossil record's apparent indication of the sudden extinction of species and the sudden emergence of new ones.

Even after three decades of accumulating evidence which points towards the Hoyle/Wickramasinghe thesis of biological activity in the Universe, the mainstream scientific community has still to come round to accepting the alternative models which, if vindicated, would cause upheavals of a revolutionary nature in not only astronomy but in biology, medicine and a range of other scientific disciplines.

V

The Scientific Legacy of Fred Hoyle:

by Sargent, L.W. W. et al.

This book, like the memorial meeting upon which it is based, is a fitting tribute to the twentieth century's greatest cosmologist. The Forward, written by the Astronomer Royal, Lord Rees, provides a general overview of the life and work of Fred Hoyle. Each of the twelve chapters examines a particular area of research in which Hoyle was engaged at different stages of his scientific career.

Hoyle's most outstanding achievement is undoubtedly his work on the synthesis of the elements in stars. Along with Geoffrey and Margaret Burbidge and the late Willy Fowler (the famous B2FH team !) Hoyle demonstrated how the heavier elements were synthesised from hydrogen by stellar nuclear reactions. The processes are described in minute detail by David Arnett in Chapter II and by Margaret Burbidge in Chapter XI.

One great value of "The Scientific Legacy of Fred Hoyle" is in its highlighting of the lesser known yet extremely important contributions by Hoyle in astrophysics. One of these is in the field of galaxy formation and evolution. George Efstathiou(Chapter III) amply describes Hoyle's work in this area. In the early 1940's, Hoyle worked on accretion theory with Raymond A. Lyttleton and Herman Bondi. In Chapter V, Sir Herman Bondi describes their work on accretion which examines the behaviour of a star which passes through a cloud of interstellar gas.

Chandra Wickramasinghe in Chapter VI (From dust to Life) treats on one of the Hoyle's most controversial theories, the idea that life had its origins in outer space and was brought to earth by means of comets, meteors and asteroids. Wickramasinghe's presentation of the spectral analyses of both gas clouds and the interstellar medium, convincingly argues in favour of Panspermia theory. His description of how bacteria were obtained from the Earth's stratosphere lends credibility to Hoyle's contention that many diseases and epidemics are caused by incoming bacteria from outer space.

No event in memory of Fred Hoyle would be complete without dealing with what Hoyle was most noted for - the Steady State Theory. Even after the discovery of the background microwave radiation which caused the majority in the astronomical community to ditch the Steady State Theory, Hoyle clung tenaciously to this model of the Universe and consistently rejected Big Bang cosmology. Malcolm S. Longair in Chapter VIII (Evolutionary cosmologies: then and now) takes us through the history of the development of the various competing cosmological theories and concludes by relating Sir Herman Bondi's remarks that the evolution of the extragalactic radio sources is "... a complex and lengthy story." Jayant V. Narlikar(Alternative Ideas in Cosmology - Chapter IX) strongly argues in favour of Hoyle's Steady State model of the Universe.

The theme that strongly runs through this memorial celebration of Fred Hoyle's achievements is that the man being remembered was not just years but decades ahead of his time. As Narlikar points out, many of Hoyle's theories which were considered as outlandish "...have now been assimilated into mainstream cosmology". In these days of corporate conformity and a slavish towing of the line, Hoyle must be seen as one of the giants who stood out from the crowd. Sadly, we may never see his likes again. In his Concluding Remarks (Chapter XII) Geoffrey Burbidge invited his fellow participants at the memorial meeting to ".... drink a toast to a great man whose achievements have lifted us all: to Fred Hoyle". May this humble review be my own "toast" to a man whose writings have inspired me for decades.

VI

Fred Hoyle's Universe:

by Jane Gregory

Jane Gregory's well researched book "Fred Hoyle's Universe" takes the reader through the amazing journey of the life of the greatest cosmologist of the twentieth century. This eighteen chapter book begins with the young Fred Hoyle's turbulent schooldays during which, in spite of his truancy, he acquired the sharp analytical mind that would prove to be the hallmark of his entire scientific career.

Ms Gregory relates Hoyle's contribution to the war effort, namely his work on the development of radar. Notwithstanding the main focus of Hoyle's work being directed towards the military exigencies of the time, he never lost sight of his main interest – astronomy.

In the post-war years, Hoyle re-directed his concentration back towards the astronomical sciences; Gregory explains how he made his debut with his series "The Nature of the Universe" which was broadcast on BBC radio's "The Third Programme" and later reproduced in book form. It was here that Hoyle achieved fame for his Steady State Theory which posited a challenge to the more widely accepted Super-dense Theory which Hoyle would later mockingly dub as the Big Bang, a term which in itself would enter into the stock of the commonly accepted parlance throughout the astronomical community in describing cosmological origins. Jane Gregory relates Hoyle's collaboration with Willy Fowler and Geoffrey and Margaret Burbidge in finding a new state of carbon and in developing the theory of stellar nucleosynthesis.

It was not only in the realm of serious science where Fred Hoyle operated; Jane Gregory mentions a number of the science fiction books which Hoyle wrote, many of which were co-authored with his son, Geoffrey. Fred Hoyle's first novel, "The Black Cloud," was a kind of precursor to a theory which he was later to develop with his colleague,

Chandra Wickramasinghe - a controversial theory which held that evolution operated in a cosmological rather than in a merely terrestrial dimension. Within the context of this new science of Astrobiology, Hoyle and Wickramasinghe, forayed into the biological and medical fields and ruffled not a few feathers in mainstream science by their contention that many common diseases such as the cold and influenza had their origins in outer space.

Hoyle did not refrain from entering the political arena. His book "A Decade of Decision," mentioned in Chapter 4 of Gregory's biography, highlights the issues confronting the post-war world while at the same time offering Hoyle's unique solutions to them. Hoyle devoted a lot of his time to lobbying governments for additional funding for scientific research especially in the field of astronomy. In this regard, Gregory provides a detailed account of how Hoyle struggled for government acceptance for the establishment of an Institute of Astronomy in Cambridge. We can clearly see from Gregory's account, Hoyle's immense contribution to the cause of astronomy in Great Britain.

Jane Gregory has compiled a comprehensive account of the life of Fred Hoyle. Her book provides many interesting insights into this highly controversial character who, by standing apart from conventionality, opened up whole new vistas in the field of scientific endeavour. Today, Hoyle's legacy continues with many of his "maverick" theories, slowly but surely, making their way into the hallways of acceptance of mainstream science.

PART II

Non-Fiction

Contents

I) The Nature of the Universe: *by Fred Hoyle* 21
II) A Decade of Decision: *by Fred Hoyle* 23
III) Man and Materialism: *by Fred Hoyle* 25
IV) Frontiers of Astronomy: *by Fred Hoyle* 26
V) Of Men and Galaxies: *by Fred Hoyle* 28
VI) Galaxies, Nuclei, and Quasars: *by Fred Hoyle* 31
VII) Man in the Universe: *by Fred Hoyle* 33
VIII) Astronomy: *a history of man's investigation of the universe: by Fred Hoyle* 36
IX) From Stonehenge to Modern Cosmology: *by Fred Hoyle* 38
X) Nicolaus Copernicus: *by Fred Hoyle* 41
XI) Action at a Distance in Physics and Cosmology: *by F Hoyle & J.V. Narlikar* 42
XII) Highlights in Astronomy: *by Fred Hoyle* 44
XIII) Astronomy Today: *by Fred Hoyle* 46
XIV) Astronomy and Cosmology: A Modern Course: *by Fred Hoyle* 48
XV) On Stonehenge: *by Fred Hoyle* 50
XVI) Ten Faces of the Universe: *by Fred Hoyle* 52
XVII) Energy or Extinction?: The Case for Nuclear Energy: *by Fred Hoyle* 54
XVIII) Lifecloud: The Origin of the Universe: *by Fred Hoyle and N.C. Wickramasinghe* 57
XIX) The Cosmogony of the Solar System: *by Fred Hoyle* 60
XX) Diseases from Space: *by Fred Hoyle and N. C. Wickramasinghe* 61
XXI) Common Sense in Nuclear Energy: *by Fred Hoyle and Geoffrey Hoyle* 64
XXII) The Origin of Life: *by Fred Hoyle and N. C. Wickramasinghe* 67
XXIII) The Relation of Biology to Astronomy: *by Fred Hoyle* 69
XXIV) Steady State Cosmology Revisited: *by Fred Hoyle* 71
XXV) ICE: *by Fred Hoyle* 73

XXVI) The Physics-Astronomy Frontier:
by Fred Hoyle & Jayant Narlikar 75
XXVII) Evolution from Space: *by Fred Hoyle & N. C. Wickramasinghe*.... 76
XXVIII) The Quasar Controversy Resolved: *by Fred Hoyle*.......... 78
XXIX) Space Travellers: *by Fred Hoyle & Chandra Wickramasinghe* 80
XXX) The Anglo-Australian Telescope: *by Fred Hoyle* 82
XXXI) Facts and Dogmas in Cosmology and Elsewhere:
by Fred Hoyle.......... 84
XXXII) The Intelligent Universe: *by Fred Hoyle*.......... 86
XXXIII) From Grains to Bacteria: *by Fred Hoyle and Chandra Wickramasinghe*.......... 88
XXXIV) Living Comets: *by Fred Hoyle and Chandra Wickramasinghe* ... 89
XXXV) The Origin of the Universe and the Origin of Religion: *by Fred Hoyle* 91
XXXVI) Viruses from Space: *by Fred Hoyle, Chandra Wickramasinghe and John Watkins* 94
XXXVII) Our Place in the Cosmos: *by Fred Hoyle & Chandra Wickramasinghe*.......... 96
XXXVIII) Lectures on Cosmology and Action at a Distance Electrodynamics:*by Fred Hoyle & Jayant Narlikar*.......... 98
XXXIX) Archaeopteryx: The Primordial Bird: *by Fred Hoyle & Chandra Wickramasinghe*.......... 99
XL) The Theory of Cosmic Grains: *by Fred Hoyle & N.C. Wickramasinghe*..........101
XLI) Life on Mars? A case for Cosmic Heritage? *by Fred Hoyle & Chandra Wickramasinghe*..........103
XLII) Mathematics of Evolution: *by Fred Hoyle*.......... 105
XLIII) Astronomical Origins of Life: Steps Towards Panspermia: *by F. Hoyle & N. C. Wickramasinghe* 107
XLIV) A Different Approach to Cosmology: from a Static Universe through the Big Bang towards Reality. *By Fred Hoyle, Geoffrey Burbidge and Jayant V. Narlikar*..... 109
XLV) Cosmic Life Force: The Power of Life across the Universe.*By Fred Hoyle & Chandra Wickramasinghe*..........111
XLVI) A Contradiction in the Argument of Malthus: *By Fred Hoyle & Chandra Wickramasinghe*.......... 114
XLVII) Why Neo- Darwinism Does Not Work: *By Fred Hoyle & Chandra Wickramasinghe*.......... 116

I

The Nature of the Universe:

by Fred Hoyle

It was "The Nature of the Universe" that brought Fred Hoyle to the notice of the general public. This book, published in 1950, is based upon a series of lectures on astronomy given by Fred for the Third Programme on BBC radio.

This book, as in all of his others, Hoyle speaks in a language easy for the layman to understand and comprehensible for the non-specialist.

First of all, Hoyle describes our Earth, the planet which we inhabit. He then takes us on a tour of nearby space and our closest neighbours, our moon and the planets of the solar system. He explains in clear and non-technical terms theories on how our solar system was formed from the primal dust and gas which condensed into solid and gaseous bodies billions of years ago.

Hoyle then goes on to discuss the sun and the stars in our galaxy. Again, in easy to understand terms, he explains how the sun gives out its heat and light by means of nuclear fusion processes, yet at the same time maintains itself as a stable and constant star. Hoyle explains stellar evolution and shows the course that the sun, like most other Main Sequence Stars, will take in the next few billion years before eventually swelling to Red Giant proportions and then shrinking to a Brown Dwarf when all its nuclear fuel is spent.

It was in this series of broadcasts, and the subsequent book, that Fred Hoyle brought to greater public attention his theory on the cosmological nature of the Universe. He rejected the super dense theory (now known as the Big Bang) of George Gamov and Georges Lemaitre and maintained that the Universe had no beginning and nor will it ever have an end: it has, he argued, always existed. As the galaxies speed away from each other into infinity, hydrogen atoms are constantly being created to replenish the Universe with new stars and galaxies. This he termed the Steady State Theory by means of continuous creation.

"The Nature of the Universe" may appear to be dated, yet it is a classic for all time as it brought to wider public awareness the new cosmology and Man's place in the Universe.

II

A Decade of Decision:

by Fred Hoyle

Fred Hoyle's book, A Decade of Decision, was written over half a century ago in 1950, and although some of its contents are dated, the bulk of the material can still be seen as being applicable to present-day problems which affect humanity.

Hoyle discussed the post-war situation in Britain and found that there was very little difference between the main political parties - Conservative and Labour. He held that elections were fought on trivia not on issues of substance. Sixty five years on, this situation has not really changed. Observers of the current political scene in Britain in the opening years of the 21st. century who are as astute as Hoyle was would realise that the differences which separate the mainstream parties in Britain today are issues of minor detail.

Hoyle examined the taxation policy of government and concluded that taxation was more than just a revenue raising devise. Revenue raised from taxation went far beyond the expenditure needs of government. Hoyle claimed that the central purpose of this heavy taxation was to make goods artificially high so as to suppress domestic consumption. Manufactured articles would be thus directed to the export market rather than the home market, the final goal in this exercise being the improvement in the nation's Balance of Payments account.

In the third chapter of this work, Hoyle examined the issue of Communism. He warned his readers that great caution had to be exercised when discussing this emotive issue. He argued that the situation as it pertained in the Soviet Union at the time was not "communism" but "russianism". His thesis was that the Soviet Union operated a virtual slave economy as its economic state of development had not yet reached the level necessary for the operation of free market capitalism. This thesis seems to be borne out in the collapse of the Soviet system in the 1990's and its change from state corporatism to free enterprise capitalism.

In the final part of his book, Hoyle examined the rise of humanity from early times to the present day. Mankind as a species really took off when nomadic groups of hunter-gatherers formed themselves into settled communities based on agriculture. This made civilisation and scientific advancement possible.

Although civilisations come and go, Hoyle saw this as being merely of a cosmetic nature. Hoyle termed this phenomenon "the civilisational cycle". The crucial factor in the survival of mankind he claimed is knowledge. As long as knowledge survives, mankind will. Civilisations may decline but resources remain the same. It is only when knowledge is lost that resources decline.

On the issue of democracy, Hoyle pointed out that there has never been a time in history when democracy arose out of a situation of chaos. This is something our political planners in the opening years of the 21st century ought to be aware of.

Finally, Fred Hoyle speculated on the future for Mankind. He saw a danger of civilisation being completely destroyed due to a decline in the non-renewable mineral resources that complex societies depend upon. Not only would civilisation be destroyed but mankind as a species could revert back to barbarism and eventually become extinct. However, Hoyle saw hope for Mankind, but only if there should ever be a greater application of the brain power of Man in the area of human relations.

III

Man and Materialism:

by Fred Hoyle

Fred Hoyle wrote his book "Man and Materialism" back in 1957, yet much of what he says can be seen as relevant to the present day. Although Hoyle was an astrophysicist, he showed great insights into political and social matters.

Although the world at the time was going through a very severe Cold War, Hoyle put the situation into a rational perspective by warning against seeing too sharp a distinction between Communism and Capitalism. Although Hoyle argued that the Capitalist system was more efficient, he showed that much of what we term as "communism" had nothing to do with the basic concept of that creed.

In the later chapters of this work, Hoyle examines the history of civilisations from the earliest history to the present day. According to Hoyle knowledge is more durable than any particular civilisation, and while civilisations wax and wane, come and go, knowledge does not. So when one civilisation collapses another can quickly arise Phoenix like from the ashes - provided knowledge is not lost.

At the conclusion of this work, Hoyle speculates about the future of Mankind. He sees a bleak future for our species if there is no alternative found to fossil fuel which he maintains will very quickly reach depletion levels. However, if nothing stands as a barrier to advancing knowledge, then Mankind may have a long future ahead.

IV

Frontiers of Astronomy:

by Fred Hoyle

Professor W. H. McCrea, in his review of "Frontiers of Astronomy" in the Spectator in 1955 wrote that "For its significance in the progress of thought it may be ranked with, say, Charles Darwin's 'Origin of Species'...His book marks a turning point in our understanding of the physical universe". Yet, Darwin's "Origin of Species" 148 years after its publication is still in print, whereas Fred Hoyle's "Frontiers of Astronomy" 52 years after its appearance in the bookshops is no longer available except through antiquarian book-dealers.

There seems to be no logical explanation for this difference in re-publication policy between the two books. Both biology and astronomy have moved on in leaps and bounds since the respective first impressions of "Origins" and "Frontiers". In fact, "Frontiers" is far more relevant to astronomy in the opening years of the 21st century than is "Origins" to biology. It could be argued that the discovery of cosmic background radiation by Dennis Sciama and Robert Wilson in 1965 has done less damage to Hoyle's Steady State theory than has been done to Darwinian evolution by Watson and Crick's discovery of DNA in the 1950's.

Perhaps the enduring success of Darwin's "Origin of Species" can be put down to the great controversy it caused not only in the scientific community but in the religious establishment itself. Neither Steady State nor Big Bang cosmology has had the same earth shattering consequences that Evolutionary Theory had.

If we take a tour of Hoyle's great work, we should come to the conclusion that controversy alone is not a rational reason for a book's endurance. Though the book is about astronomy, Hoyle devotes the first two chapters of "Frontiers" to planet Earth. Some commentators have viewed this as being rather odd but we must come to the realisation that

Earth is no less a part of the Universe than is the Andromeda Galaxy. Throughout his career Hoyle was constantly criticised for stepping into disciplines in which he had no training. Hoyle countered this criticism by explaining that nature does not categorise in the way academe does; there is always going to be overlapping among the sciences. It makes no sense whatsoever to suggest that an astronomer can pronounce on the rock composition and the weather patterns on Mars but only a geologist and a meteorologist can have anything relevant to say respectively on Earth's rocks and climates!

The concept of overlap continues in chapters III and IV as Hoyle takes his readers down into the microcosmic world of the atom and explains the nature of sub-atomic particles. It is impossible to attain any grasp of how the Universe functions in its vastness without a proper understanding of what is going on at the atomic and sub-atomic levels. Microcosm and macrocosm are inextricably bound up.

It is only from chapter V that we leave the Earth to begin a study of the moon, the planets and our nearest star the sun. As we progress through the remaining 15 chapters we find ourselves taken further out into deep space as we consider the origins of the solar system and examine the various types of stars in our galaxy. Moving onwards Hoyle fascinates us with the different kinds of galaxies and their enormous distances in an expanding Universe.

Hoyle concludes his work by giving an outline of the Steady State Theory and its adjunct theory of the continuous creation of matter. The Steady State Theory's non-viability in its original form puts it on a par with Darwinian Evolutionary Theory thus raising the hope one day we may witness "Frontiers of Astronomy" and "Origin of Species" separated on the bookshelvesonly by the academic labels of "biology" and "astronomy".

V

Of Men and Galaxies:

by Fred Hoyle

In 1961, John and Jesse Danz made a substantial gift to the University of Washington to establish a fund to provide income to be used to bring to the university each year "....distinguished scholars of national and international reputation who have concerned themselves with the impact of science and philosophy on Man's perception of the rational Universe." It was as a "John Danz Lecturer" that Fred Hoyle delivered a series of lectures in 1964 entitled "Of Men and Galaxies" and published his lectures in book form under the same title.

This book like all of Hoyle's earlier writings, it is still highly relevant to the opening years of the 21st. century. I first read this book over fifty years ago - in 1964; I re-read it forty years later in 2004, and I realised that nothing has changed in all that time. Nowadays, this book can only be obtained from the dusty stacks of university libraries or in the dark recesses of shops dealing in antiquarian publications. However, I believe this book is a must for not only scientists, but for social scientists and politicians - in fact for all those concerned about the future direction of the human species.

In the field of science, Hoyle pointed out that the great scientific breakthroughs of the twentieth century were achieved with equipment which cost only a few hundred dollars. Since the middle of the same century, equipment has run into hundreds and even thousands of millions of dollars. This has stifled the work of the scientist as he now has to spend as much time lobbying government for funds, sitting on committees and thus engaging himself in masses of bureaucratic minutiae as in scientific research and development. The main point Hoyle made was that in the past, the great men and women associated with great discoveries did not depend on "big science", they depended on big ideas. Scientists therefore are overawed by the large equipment, the large buildings which contain them and the large bureaucracies which administer them. This "bigness" forces the scientist into a conventional mind-set and establishment strait-jacket. Hoyle called it the dinosaur mentality. Yet, Hoyle had hope, as "... it is in the nature of dinosaurs to reach an end, to become extinct". It is impossible for machines to be built on ever larger scales ad infinitum for the simple reason that the totality of human effort cannot be exceeded. Therefore the solution lies in astronomy and astrophysics. Phenomena in our galaxy and beyond can attain temperatures of thousands, millions and in extreme cases even billions of degrees centigrade - conditions which cannot be replicated in the terrestrial laboratory. Therefore the Universe ought to be seen as one large laboratory. This way, the line between physics and astrophysics becomes blurred and a field of fruitful co-operation can be opened up between the terrestrial scientist and the astronomer.

In the second lecture, Fred Hoyle considered the possibility of creating an artificial human being. If the right atoms and molecules were synthesised and were made to fit together in the right order, an artificial human being could be created. Nevertheless, this would not necessarily mean that the manufactured human being would behave and function like a real human being, even though chemically the synthetic human being would be similar. Creating an artificial human is more than just putting the right atoms in the right place, the state of the atom is also relevant, and it is there where the greatest difficulty would arise.

Hoyle then speculated upon the possibility of life elsewhere in the galaxy - particularly intelligent life. He considered ways in which intelligent life forms like our own could be contacted. Actual interstellar space travel he considered to be impossible due to the immense distances involved, but communication would most likely be made by radio and television signals sent across intergalactic space. Civilisations could learn much from each other by making contact, and it was by this means that a vast accumulation of knowledge might be built up. It was with this process in mind that Hoyle coined the phrase "the galactic library" - perhaps nowadays we might call it "the galactic internet".! One of the great benefits of such knowledge would be in learning from civilisations older than our own, how to avoid the catastrophe of nuclear war and global annihilation.

In his third and final lecture, Fred takes us down to earth with a thump and considers the problems of population growth on the planet. The increase in population is having a negative impact on the aesthetic quality of life, large cities are overcrowded and impersonal places - the small village and township community is to be preferred. The places on Planet Earth where one can "get away from it all" are becoming fewer and fewer.

Hoyle then examines these problems within a political context. He emphasised the fact that no political party has ever fought an election on the real issues which profoundly touch people's quality of life - "increase in privacy, less crowding in cities, smaller communities, and, above all, less pressure in our everyday lives". Instead, elections are fought and won on trivial issues.

So where are we fifty years down the road? The scenery looks much the same; big science still reigns supreme, and the substantial issues arising out of overpopulation are still politically sidelined in favour of trivialities. That is why I think the book should be re-issued and studied by those who may have it in their power to change things for the better. What about the next fifty years? We can only hope against hope that the powers-that-be will prioritise what has been sidelined, and sideline what has been wrongly prioritised. Let us hope and pray that the dinosaurs which Fred Hoyle warned of will have become extinct.

VI

Galaxies, Nuclei, and Quasars:

by Fred Hoyle

Fred Hoyle published "Galaxies, Nuclei, and Quasars" in 1965 and discussed in that work the discoveries and developments in astronomy that had taken place over the previous decade. Hoyle himself had played a major part in the great advances made in astronomical science throughout the 1950's and 1960's.

As in all his works, Hoyle lays out an easy to understand approach to the astronomical phenomena he presents, an approach which is essential for a layman's understanding of it. He begins by explaining the structures of galaxies, the huge "islands of stars" of which the Universe is mainly composed. Hoyle explains that not all galaxies have the same shape, structure or size, but that they nevertheless do fall within a certain limited range of classification types.

Until the late 1940's, astronomy had been mainly an optical science. But one of the spin-offs of the technological advances in the Second World War, was the radio telescope. With the construction of Jodrell Bank, radio astronomy as a branch of astronomy really came into its own. Sir Bernard Lovell was a great pioneer in this field. Hoyle explains very clearly the different types of radio sources in the Universe, many of which cannot be identified with optical telescopes.

Hoyle then discusses the mysterious cosmic rays which permeate the Universe and considers a number of theories regarding their origin. Like radio telescopy, cosmic ray astronomy, said Hoyle, is also a means by which the Universe can be explored.

No book written by Fred Hoyle would be complete without a discussion of the Steady State Theory. This is very much Hoyle's "calling card" as he consistently argued against Big Bang cosmology. The

Universe, he contended, has always existed and always will as the laws of physics never came into being at any particular moment in time.

Whether or not one accepts Hoyle's cosmological model of the Universe, "Galaxies, Nuclei, and Quasars" is a fascinating read and very profitable not only for the amateur astronomer, but also for a science student who has the hope of eventually specialising in astronomy.

VII

Man in the Universe:

by Fred Hoyle

"Man in the Universe" was published in 1966 by Columbia University Press. The book is based upon the 17th of the Bampton series of lectures which was delivered by Fred Hoyle at Columbia University in the USA in 1964. This hardback consists of 81 pages and is divided into five chapters.

"Man in the Universe" is rather similar to Hoyle's other book "Of men and galaxies" which was based upon the John Danz lectures delivered by Hoyle in 1964. These books look at Man's place in the Universe and how both Man and Universe relate to each other.

In the first chapter of "Man in the Universe", Fred Hoyle makes a critical examination of the space programme in terms of its relationship to astronomy. His basic thesis is that the former has no relevance to the latter and that the money spent upon space research would be more productively invested in ground based astronomical equipment. It could possibly be argued that the Hubble Space Telescope has now rendered Hoyle's criticism of the space programme redundant, but before we be too hasty in dismissing Hoyle on account of Hubble there are two considerations which need be kept in mind: first of all Hoyle foresaw telescopes in space and space stations orbiting the Earth. Secondly, Hoyle did acknowledge that space telescopes would make major contributions in the field of astronomy. However, Hoyle predicted that the bulk of the advancements in astronomy would still emanate from ground based equipment. When we examine the history of the Hubble telescope, we come to realise that Hoyle has very much been vindicated in his analysis. Hubble indeed has made groundbreaking discoveries but this telescope's successors are not, so far, other space telescopes, but terrestrially based astronomical equipment.

In the second chapter, entitled "know then thyself", Hoyle discusses the difference between Man's perception of the Universe through the eyes of religion and through the eyes of science. He argues that Man's religious conditioning has prevented him from "seeing the obvious". In this regard, Hoyle contends, the great breakthrough came in the nineteenth century with Darwin's and Wallace's discoveries that showed Man to be an animal. Hoyle pointed out that he was not attacking religion as he believed the same blinkers prevent Man today from engaging in the kind of original thought necessary for his advancement. Many people have what Hoyle calls "flashes" of originality. Some of these flashes are rubbish, others are brilliant. The trick is to sort out one from the other. Hoyle saw this as no easy matter; essentially he identified two types of person in this regard - on the one hand, the crank who holds on to his original ideas in spite of overwhelming evidence of the un-workability of them, and on the other, the most scientific and technically competent who see too readily the problems associated with their workable original ideas and thus over-hastily abort them at inception. Throughout the rest of this chapter and into the third (entitled "the subjective present") Hoyle presents his readers with his own flashes and insights into modern physics, most particularly Quantum Theory and its relationship to consciousness.

In the penultimate chapter of this book, Hoyle puts education and research under the microscope. The burgeoning of education (what today we might call "the education industry") he sees as a means by which governments ensure against the extremes of alternating economic boom and slump. Hoyle identified the modern student as one who saw education as being a "meal-ticket". By this he meant that the majority of modern students see no intrinsic value in the subjects they are studying but instead view their studies and exams merely as means to an end - the end being employment. Hoyle argued for the complete revamping of the educational system, a revamping based upon the neurological biology of a child. He contended that language learning should begin at a very young age due to the fact that linguistic ability decreases with a child's advancing years. He viewed mathematical and scientific ability in the same light and gave convincing evidence that young children should concentrate mainly on these in their formative years. Subjects such as history and literature should only be introduced when the child achieves a greater emotional maturity in order to understand better human characteristics such as love, hate and jealousy which are dealt with in the study of these subjects.

In the final chapter "the poetry of Earth is never dead", Fred Hoyle asks the most profound question of all - what as a species are we doing on this planet? Surely there can be no doubt that the answer to this question can indicate to us exactly what our place is in the Universe. Hoyle bemoaned the fact that too few people have the time or indeed perspective to consider such a lofty question. He claimed that only if we develop a clear understanding between the individual and the community can mankind make progress in the future. Hoyle noted that the morale of communities correlates to great individual achievement. Yet, when research proposals are made, the inevitable question asked is "Does it have any use?". However, Hoyle goes further and asks "What is meant by use?" Sadly it is, according to Hoyle, whatever ".... serves to make the most machines, the more machines, the more the use". Our long term success as a species cannot be based upon technology. The human species must collectively come to see that its true destiny lies in "....perception, in understanding the universal game that is going on around us, the game of which we are perhaps a tiny part."

All of Hoyle's books are as relevant today as they were at the time they were written and "Man in the Universe" offers no exception in this regard.

VIII

Astronomy:

a history of man's investigation of the universe: by Fred Hoyle

"Astronomy" with the subtitle "a history of man's investigation of the universe," is a beautifully illustrated bumper seven inch by ten and a half inch book by Fred Hoyle. As it is essentially a history of the development of astronomy since the earliest times in the history of mankind, Hoyle tackles the oft asked question as to the usefulness and purpose of the astronomical sciences. The author brilliantly answers the critics by succinctly pointing out that astronomy is the oldest of all the sciences, and yet, the newest of the sciences (p.6). Without astronomy, travel would have been impossible as the points of the compass would never have been established and astro-navigation would never have been devised. Were the Earth a cloud covered planet, with no window looking out on to the celestial sphere, the very concept of time itself could never have been developed. Euclidean geometry, and other areas of mathematics on which so much of science depends would likewise have remained beyond the grasp of humanity's common intellect. (pp. 10 – 12).

In the second chapter of the book, the author walks us through the development of the instrumentation used by man in his attempts at understanding the heavens. While Hoyle explains a variety of time measuring instruments from the simplest of sundials to the great telescopes, such as those located on Mounts Wilson and Palomar, we learn that a number of the objects we use in our everyday lives for time measurement, such as the common clock, the wrist watch and the calendar, are all, in a sense, astronomical instruments.

In the third chapter, Hoyle examines the development of celestial astronomy from ancient times to the present day. He explains the difference between the Greek geometrical approach to the motions of the heavenly bodies and the Babylonian approach in which the movements of the moon and the apparent motions of the sun and stars were interwoven into the culture. Hoyle goes on to relate how Copernicus, Brahe, Kepler and Galileo arrived at the true motion of the Earth around a heliocentric solar system (Ch.4).

It is in its relation to the physical sciences that astronomy is the newest of the sciences. In chapter 6 the author goes on to explain how men like Newton and Huygens introduced gravitational theory in the understanding of planetary motion. In order to determine the nature and composition of the sun and stars, it was necessary to discover the properties of light. Chapter 7 tackles the issue of how spectroscopic instrument development greatly increased our knowledge of what astronomical phenomena are made. Chapters 8 and 9 develop the theme of modern day astronomy by elucidating the different types of stars, their composition, their nuclear synthetic processes and their evolution.

Hoyle explains galactic structure and formation in Chapter 10 of the book. He also discourses upon the planets and other bodies in the solar system and offers a theory as to their formation from a disc of material ejected from the sun. Hoyle concludes his great work by taking a broad view of the Universe as a whole (Ch. 11) and weighing up the evidence for and against the two contending theories of cosmic origin - the Superdense Theory (or "Big Bang") and the one consistently favoured by Hoyle, the Steady State Theory.

Although the astronomical sciences have come a long way since this book was published in 1968, it remains an extremely useful work for those who would wish to obtain a solid grounding in the progress and development of astronomy and see the astronomical sciences within the greater context of humanity's unceasing march towards an ever more sophisticated future in scientific and technological advance.

IX

From Stonehenge to Modern Cosmology:

by Fred Hoyle

From Stonehenge to Modern Cosmology is based upon four lectures delivered by Fred Hoyle under the auspices of the Distinguished Visiting Series organised by the California Institute of Technology circa 1970. In the first of these lectures, Hoyle makes a highly interesting comparison between two extremes of scientific era which would apparently defy any attempts at comparison, yet, thanks to Hoyle's brilliant analytical abilities, the comparison is made transparent by means of a sharp and penetrating insight for which Hoyle has always been distinguished. Hoyle demonstrates by mathematical and observational techniques that Stonehenge was an ancient astronomical observatory, and its being so, serves to rank Stone Age Man in a higher category of scientific knowledge and achievement than the one into which he is generally placed by consensus historical and archeological consensus.

The construction of Stonehenge "....must have consumed a considerable fraction of the productivity of the whole community". It is within the context of this observation that Hoyle demonstrates that within Stone Age society, Stonehenge is equivalent to the largest instruments of the particle physicist in the modern era, instruments whose worth is within the region of $100,000,000. Hoyle goes on to examine the relationship between scientists and the communities within which they operate and notes that the latter do not have an easy time of it. This is in stark contrast to the builders of Stonehenge. Hoyle's explanation for this is that the builders of Stonehenge were closer to their communities than modern day scientists in that they provided the sort of tangible results that tend to evade modern scientific achievement within modern day communities. In his various other writings, Hoyle has frequently bemoaned the fact that scientists are essentially excluded from the decision making processes of society, these being the sole prerogative of the technically and scientifically unqualified. Yet, here Hoyle seems to have given a subliminal answer to this seemingly societal flaw - the distrust by many in the community of science and scientists, and the scarcity of what he terms "tangible results" in scientific development. Yet, this could well be the fault of society. Hoyle highlights the fact that many scientists, even within the relatively sheltered walls of a university, are snowed under with bureaucratic tasks and governmental administrative requirements which have no relevance to scientific research and discovery. It would appear that at this juncture Hoyle contradicts himself by claiming that the ideal situation for a scientist in which to operate most effectively is one of distance from society, whereas he had previously lauded the builders of Stonehenge for being closer to the societies in which they operated. However, when we once more consider the greater degree of "tangible results" from the Stone Age builders of Stonehenge, we realise a greater overlap must have existed then between these early scientists and their community than exists between modern day scientists and their communities.

Hoyle provides his readers with a very interesting perspective on religion by arguing that Stonehenge was indeed built for religious purposes. However, it is not of the kind of religious rites and rubrics of which we are most accustomed to today. Instead Hoyle argues that the scientific discovery of the beauty of the laws of nature and the structure of the Universe are genuine forms of religion, and it was with these religious concepts in mind that Stone Age Man on Salisbury Plain proceeded with the construction of Stonehenge.

It is interesting to note Hoyle's claim that the Stone Age's giving way to the Bronze Age caused astronomical science to suffer a set-back in that communal productive effort became concentrated on the smelting of metal. It is no doubt with this fact in mind that Hoyle makes the fascinating assertion that the builders of Stonehenge and their community were far ahead of the civilisations of the Middle East and even those of Greece and Rome.

Though it is forty five years since the publication of this work, its ideas are still controversial and thus subject to heated debate. "Archaeo-astronomy" which Hoyle did so much to found is an academic field ripe for future investigation and research. Hoyle saw the likes of Stonehenge as providing far greater solidity of historical evidence than the documents which conventional historians are wont to use. Future researchers in this area may well take this book as their starting point for their investigations.

X

Nicolaus Copernicus:

by Fred Hoyle

What makes Fred Hoyle's work on Nicolaus Copernicus so interesting is that it does not despise the old Ptolemaic theory of a geocentric universe. "Indeed Copernicus had to struggle long and hard over many years before he equaled Ptolemy, and in the end the Copernican theory did not greatly surpass that of Ptolemy" (P. 3) Hoyle points out in many places throughout this work, that in pure terms of kinematic models, it is immaterial whether one uses the heliocentric or geocentric forms of representation.

Hoyle gives a brief account of Copernicus' personal life in Chapter II. He traces Copernicus' career from his birth in Silesia in 1473 to his death in Frauenburg in 1543. The development of Copernicus' heliocentric model is carefully investigated from the first publication "Commentariolus" to its culmination in "de revolutionibus".

In the other two chapters of the book, Hoyle examines in mathematical terms the heliocentric theory of Aristarchus and the Copernican and Ptolemaic models of the solar system. In the epilogue, which looks at the two models with respect to the 20th century, Hoyle states that one cannot say that the "....Copernican theory is `right' and the Ptolemaic theory `wrong'....". It is simply that using the Ptolemaic model rather than the Copernican one would have been futile within any desire to make scientific progress.

XI

Action at a Distance in Physics and Cosmology:

by F. Hoyle & J.V. Narlikar

Action at a Distance in Physics and Cosmology by Fred Hoyle and Professor Jayant V. Narlikar is an extremely technical book and not really intended for the general lay reader. Its complex mathematical equations can really only enter the realm of understanding of a student with a background in physics. Those however, who are trained in this discipline, will find the book extremely rewarding.

In the preface to this work, the authors explain the term "action at a distance" as being "......a relativistically invariant particle interaction, not the instantaneous action at a distance of Newton". In physics it is customary that interaction is used in some problems such as scattering, the general viewpoint being that inter-particle action is merely part of a wider interaction of fields and particles. The authors challenge this conventional view by arguing that all the results of physics "....can be obtained from inter-particle action - for decay problems and scattering problems alike".

Hoyle and Narlikar go on to challenge another scientific conventionality which holds that the universe sets boundary conditions for the working of the laws of physics and that these laws act independently of large scale structure and could be discovered by local experimentation. Hoyle and Narlikar however argue in favour of a seamless garment for the laws of physics at local and universal levels.

Chapter 2, which deals with the theories of electromagnetism and gravitation, place theoretical physics within an historical perspective by explaining that such diverse phenomena as the swings of a pendulum, a falling apple and planetary motion all adhere to the same scientific laws.

In the following chapters, the authors go on to expound on Gauss's problem and how it was solved in the early 20th century by Schwarzschild, Tetrode and Fokker. As nature is quantum in character, classical particle physics is insufficient for the explanation of any physical theory, so the authors place electromagnetism within quantum theory. In chapter 5, Hoyle and Narlikargeneralise the Fokker action to curved spacetime.

The book's authors succeed in obtaining a quantum generalisation of the electrodynamic case and how this leads "....to extension of the action at a distance point of view to all parts of physics." However, the authors admit that "...other major issues remain.....especially those related to short-range forces".

XII

Highlights in Astronomy:

by Fred Hoyle

Highlights in Astronomy was written by Fred Hoyle in 1974. The book is well illustrated with photographs and graphs and ends with a section for questions and discussions on the various astronomical topics dealt with in the book.

There are eight chapters in the book. The first chapter examines the Earth in terms of its place in the solar system and its geological and biological aspects. Chapter 2 looks at the solar system with regard to its kinematics and the historical processes which combined to construct the heliocentric model by which we understand the motions of the sun and planets today. In the next chapter, Hoyle goes on to examine the planets themselves and compares and contrasts their various sizes and composition. In chapter 4, the author explains the nuclear processes by which the sun gives off radiation in the form of light and heat while the following chapter examines the nature of comets and what Hoyle terms "astronomical debris" - material left over from the discharge of comets and from the time of the formation of the solar system. Hoyle then goes on to look at stars and considers how they are formed, their various sizes and types and their life span. In the penultimate chapter, the author looks at perhaps the greatest mystery of all time - life in the Universe. He considers the number of possible habitable abodes in the galaxy for life as we know it, and ponders the question of how contact could be made with civilizations in the galaxy. Hoyle avers that contact can only be made if technological civilisations do not annihilate themselves after a 10,000 year period. The final chapter introduces us to the truly vast expanse of the Universe and the incredible distances between galaxies. Hoyle discusses the greatest of all questions - where did it all come from and what is the meaning of it? Fred Hoyle, throughout his life, consistently steered clear of adopting the general Big bang consensus, instead, opting for an interpretation of cosmological phenomena within a Steady State framework.

Highlights In Astronomy is a highly readable book. It assumes no prior knowledge of Astronomy and explains in clear layman's language the structure and functioning the Universe and Mankind's place within it.

XIII

Astronomy Today:

by Fred Hoyle

In the preface to "Astronomy Today", the author, Fred Hoyle makes the following apropos statement: 'In the very troubled times in which we are living today, astronomy offers a welcome new perspective on a scheme of things much larger than ourselves'. This is as true today as it was back in 1974 when Hoyle wrote this book. When contemplating the immense vastness of the cosmos and simultaneously coming to a realisation of the minuteness of the Earth within it, we become more conscious of the need for the greater part of humanity to achieve a greater awareness of just how the petty politicking which absorbs so much of our collective time, energy and passions sooner or later must be put into a more realistic perspective. In its non-technical, easy to understand terminology, "Astronomy Today" undoubtedly offers a major contribution to the growth and development of that cosmic consciousness on whose evolution and maturity depend the continuation of the existence of the human species - at least in terms of how it is represented on planet Earth.

It is on Earth where Hoyle begins his journey and examines our planet's geological, biological and climatic history. On commenting upon the first of the astonishing pictures in this well-illustrated book, the author amazes at how it was that the animal who was responsible for these extraterrestrial photographs was the one which, weighed down by the force of gravity, evolution never favoured with the ability of flight!

In the following two chapters we move out from the Earth towards the planets and the sun. Hoyle clearly shows how humanity's consciousness changed from a geocentric view of the Universe to one which embraced heliocentrism - a model which placed the sun at the centre of the cosmos. He looks at the planets one by one and explains their varying sizes, atmospheric compositions and geological make-up. The sun, by far the largest body in our solar system, is given a chapter all to itself in which is described the solar atmosphere and various other features such as flares, sunspots and the solar wind and how these affect the Earth in terms of climate and magnetic storms. The author finishes his tour of the solar system by considering other phenomena such as comets, meteors and various forms of debris which "litter" the space between the planets.

In the final three chapters of the book, Hoyle moves out of the solar system and considers the stars. This book comes with sky charts showing the constellations and a list of the constellation names and their positions in the sky during the summer and winter seasons. The author goes on to explain star formation and the life-cycles of stars from their birth in hot clouds of interstellar gas and dust to the end of their lives as neutron stars and black holes.

Hoyle considers one of the greatest of all questions - life elsewhere in the Universe. While he accepts that there may be life forms we are totally unaware of, he comments that this is very much in the realms of speculation. However, there is no reason given the vastness of the Universe why carbon based life should not have arisen on planets suitable for biological evolution. Hoyle notes though that contacting any intelligent life in the galaxy would present very serious technological challenges.

In the final chapter, the author discusses varying types of galaxies and their formation. In contemplating the Universe as a whole, Hoyle states that what the furthest limits of our current astronomical equipment permits us to observe may only be a tiny fraction of an ever much larger Universe. The book ends with a section devoted to questions and topics for discussions based upon each of the eight chapters of the book.

XIV

Astronomy and Cosmology: A Modern Course:

by Fred Hoyle

"Astronomy and Cosmology – A modern course", covers everything that a beginner in the science of astronomy needs in order to get a grasp of the fundamentals of this vast field of study. It is a huge volume of over 700 pages, and although written in 1975, the basic tenets of astronomy remain largely unchanged, so the student of 2015 will find Fred Hoyle's course book just as much an invaluable guide to his studies as his predecessor of the 1970's did.

The book is organised into six main divisions with further sections and subsections within these divisions. Throughout each section, the author gives the student problems to solve; these are related to the particular topic of the section. At the end of each division, there are a large number of problems and questions for the student to tackle. Hoyle is quite the task-master cracking the whip - there will be no slacking on the part of the students!

Hoyle's course book is comprehensive in that it covers practically all aspects of astronomy. The first division deals with the celestial sphere as seen from a terrestrial perspective, and extremely useful star charts and tables showing respectively the shapes and names of the constellations are provided. These sections deal with the solar system, our galaxy, other galaxies and the general structure of the Universe.

The second division of the book takes a look at the practical side of astronomy and examines the tools and instruments used by astronomers in the course of their work.

The third division takes the reader from the macro to the micro by showing the connection between astronomy and the structure of the atom. In this part of the book, the student will come to understand the interrelatedness of atomic structure and the Universe and how it is that astronomical phenomena requires the concepts of physics for their explanation and elucidation. At this point, it behooves the reviewer to advise the would-be astronomer, that a good grounding in mathematics is essential for a full understanding of astronomical data.

The fourth division of the book examines theories regarding the origin of the solar system and goes on to consider the great question as to whether or not life exists elsewhere in the Universe.

Radio-astronomy is dealt with in the fifth division of the book, and in division six the wider aspect of cosmology considers the origin of the Universe and looks at the rival big bang and steady state models.

So much has happened in astronomy since 1975, but I would aver that Fred Hoyle's course book still constitutes a must for those who want to get to grips with the essentials of astronomy.

XV

On Stonehenge:

by Fred Hoyle

Almost everyone knows Stonehenge, but so very few people know what it is. If you were to ask the average man on the Clapham Omnibus the question, "what is Stonehenge?" he would probably answer something in the way of its being an ancient monument of stones serving purely ritualistic purposes connected to the religious rites of the Neolithic society which constructed it.

In his book "On Stonehenge," Fred Hoyle gives a completely different interpretation of the structure and shows by meticulous observation and careful calculation, that Stonehenge was nothing less than an astronomical observatory designed essentially to predict eclipses of the sun.

Generally it is hard for most people to accept that Stone Age man could have possessed such complex astronomical knowledge. In keeping an open mind as to the interpretation of Stonehenge, Hoyle counsels that we must shed all prejudices in this regard and proceed on a basis which accords solely with the evidence. Whilst work on the structure commenced around 2,500BC, mankind, says Hoyle, had most likely been observing the motions of the heavens for 10,000 years and so would have been quite aware of the celestial structure and the movements of its parts.

One of the most interesting insights of this work of Hoyle's is how the discipline of astronomy connects with that of pre-history. As Hoyle points out in his book, pre-historians obtain their data from below ground level by means of archaeological digs, and thus tend to slant pre-historical knowledge around the funerary aspects of ancient societies. However, the mathematical and astronomical abilities of those who lived in the pre-historical era can be elicited by the engagement of present day science in studies in the pre-historical arena. Hoyle makes the interesting observation - "The intellectual activity of mankind during pre-history is a vast, almost uncharted ocean" (p.115). In ancient societies, religion and science would have been more intertwined than they are in the modern era, key points in the year being calculated by the positioning of the stones of Stonehenge in relation to the sun, moon and stars, would have been rendered religious expression in the way of ritual and colourful festivals as celebratory of the seasons. Hoyle visualised ".....dancers appearing on the festival days, a vision very different from the grimmer mortuary reports of the archaeologist" (p.131).

XVI

Ten Faces of the Universe:

by Fred Hoyle

As the title of the book suggests, Fred Hoyle looks at the Universe from ten different perspectives. The first chapter is entitled "God's Universe" and it is here that Hoyle displays his familiar dislike of conventional religious beliefs and practices. God, for Hoyle, is part of the mathematical creation which is the Universe, rather than someone who, in traditional theology, stands outside of it and apart from it.

Chapter 2 is entitled "The Physicist's Universe" and here the author looks carefully at the fundamental particles of matter of which everything is composed. Hoyle introduces the reader to the microscopic world of atoms, electrons, protons and quarks.

In "The Mathematician's Universe", which is the title of Chapter 3, Hoyle explains the four basic forces which hold the Universe together – the gravitational and electrical interactions and the weak and strong interactions.

The way the astrophysicist looks at the Universe is discussed in chapter 4. The astrophysicist applies the principle of the detailed structure of matter to the entire Universe whereas the physicist is mainly concerned with the smaller world of fundamental particles.

Chapter 6 takes a look at the expanding Universe and focuses on the large structures of which our Universe is composed. We learn here about the different types of galaxy and the mysterious objects called quasars, neutron stars and proton stars.

The great question about the origin of the Universe is discussed in the following chapter. Hoyle explains the phenomena of the microwave background radiation within an alternative context to Big Bang cosmology. In terms of particle regression in size back through time,

Hoyle demonstrates the greater plausibility of the Steady State model as an explanation for the origin of the Universe.

In the unusually named chapter "Nobody's Universe", Hoyle leads us into the strange world of Quantum Mechanics. The author introduces the reader to the fascinating concept of how human consciousness may affect the response of the physical phenomena in the Universe.

"The Geophysicist's Universe" is a chapter devoted to terrestrial geological structures and to the origin of the solar system while the penultimate chapter deals with the origin of life on Earth and the possibility of life forms existing throughout the Universe and how we may get in contact with the places on which it may have developed to a high level of intelligence.

The final chapter, "Everyman's Universe" deals with the great issues facing humanity both now and in the future. Hoyle identifies these problems as rising population and the inability to provide sufficient supplies of energy to meet the increase in demand. Hoyle predicted that the problem would reach a crisis point by 2025; it is in this sense that "The Ten Faces of the Universe" is as relevant now as it was when it was written in 1977 as, at the present time of writing this review, 2025 is only 10 years away!

XVII

Energy or Extinction?: The Case for Nuclear Energy:

by Fred Hoyle

As I write this review, the price of oil hovers at around the $50 per barrel mark. With demand on the verge of outstripping supply, it seems to be the case that the cost of a barrel of oil will be adjusted upwards rather than downwards as the months and the years role by. Newspaper editorials and television and radio newsreel analyses of the current energy crisis concentrate on mainly two aspects of the problem - the politically volatile situation in the Middle East and the need to explore for oil in more remote parts of the world. Very few commentators in the media have managed to get a handle on the crux of the matter which is that hydrocarbons are now reaching depletion levels.

In the final chapter of his book "Energy or Extinction? The Case for Nuclear Energy" Fred Hoyle criticised a Sunday Times article of 12th December 1976 in which the author persuasively argued the case for delaying Britain's nuclear energy programme on the basis that "we have time". Hoyle directly contradicted this statement by asserting that "we do not have time". Those who are aware that the phase the world is now entering into with regard to hydrocarbons is more geological than it is political will be astonished at Hoyle's astuteness in being able to predict the problem as far back as 1976. Yet, even more astonishingly, Hoyle's foresight concerning the depletion of hydrocarbons goes back even further. In his books "Man and Materialism" and "A Decade of Decision", both published in the early 1950's, Hoyle warned that hydrocarbons afforded mankind a mere temporary breathing space and that plans to base energy on alternatives to fossil fuels should be under serious consideration by governments. In his Forward to Hoyle's book, Sir

Alan Cottrell, a one-time scientific advisor to H.M. Government stated that, with regard to nuclear power, and with especial regard to the safer non fast breeder reactor of the Canadian CANDU type "It is surely a scandal that the US and UK have ignored this attractive alternative for so long".

"Energy or Extinction" (pub. Heinemann), although a short 80 page book consisting of a forward, introduction, six chapters and an index, clearly, succinctly and persuasively lays forth the case for nuclear power as the only viable alternative to oil and coal. Fred completely debunks the scaremongering of the anti-nuclear lobby which conveys the notion that nuclear power constitutes a danger. Backing up his argument with the use of statistics, he shows that there is more radiation emanating from common rocks, coal ash and hospital x-rays than from nuclear power plants. Hoyle makes perfectly clear that driving, living in cities, and working in the construction, coal-mining, dock and textile industries are far greater hazards to life and health than the nuclear power industry.

After guiding the reader through the astrophysical processes by which the Earth came to acquire its hydrocarbons and various mineral deposits, Hoyle examines the viability of non-nuclear energy alternatives such as solar, wind and wave power and concludes that they are no substitutes for nuclear energy. To provide the world with energy based on solar power, 1% of the Earth's surface would have to be covered with solar panels - this would be an area comparable to the size of Western Europe. And collecting all the electricity from the vast array of tiny cells could never be done efficiently or inexpensively. Hoyle demonstrates how wind power is as unfeasible as solar power. If Britain were to obtain all its power from wind mills, an area half the size of England would be covered by these mills - about 20 million of them! Obtaining energy from tides and waves would, as Hoyle says, "....be an engineer's nightmare". Britain would require a coastal boom length of 8,000 miles to provide its energy needs by this method and the world would need to have a boom length of 600,000 miles.

Energy obtained from the uranium in common rocks would provide energy for at least 30,000 years. Hoyle calculates that with technological improvements in which a 50% burn up rate is achieved, the lifetime of uranium based energy could be extended to hundreds of thousands of years. Further technological refinement resulting in a higher percentage burn-up could even extend resources to millions of years. Regarding the issue of leakage from waste, Hoyle explains that the half life of various radioactive elements would eventually produce a balance in the amount of radiation from nuclear waste. Leakage from waste buried 3,000 feet underground would have lost much of its radioactivity by the time it reached the surface - if it ever did. There is more radiation in our water supply produced by rain running off the common radioactive rocks in mountains than could ever be produced by leakage.

"Energy or Extinction" was used as an Open University set book. If this book were currently widely available to those both in academe and industry who are involved in the issue of energy, there would surely be a greater sense of urgency in the development of nuclear based energy facilities. Sadly, we do not seem to have progressed beyond that 1976 Sunday Times article and are thus still deluding ourselves that "we have time".

XVIII

Lifecloud: The Origin of the Universe:

by Fred Hoyle and N.C. Wickramasinghe

"Lifecloud - The Origin of Life in the Universe" wasco-authored by Fred Hoyle and Professor Chandra Wickramasinghe. It consists of 189 pages and is divided into nineteen chapters and two appendixes.

Like all of Hoyle's and Wickramasinghe's works, "Lifecloud" is a fascinating book. Perhaps the best way to read this book is with reference to the most recent discoveries in the academic discipline of what has now become known as "astro-chemistry". When Hoyle and Wichramasinghe first proposed their theory that the origin of life had a cosmic rather than merely a terrestrial dimension, most of the scientific community pooh-poohed their ideas. At the time of writing this review, over 140 organic molecules have been detected in interstellar gas clouds in the galaxy. No astronomer now doubts that there is a lot of complex chemistry going on in outer space. It is therefore important that justice be done and that Fred Hoyle and Prof. Chandra Wickramasinghe be acknowledged as pioneers in this branch of astronomy.

In the first chapter of the book, the two authors point out that the Earth is not a closed system as around 100 or so metric tons of matter from outer space enter our planet's atmosphere every day. A certain type of meteor known as a carbonaceous chondrite is rich in organic compounds. In chapter 2 entitled "myths, miracles and the origin of life", Hoyle and Wickramasinghe demonstrate that the conditions of the primitive Earth were not conducive for life to begin. However, if prebiotic molecules are not only common throughout interstellar space and in the gas halos around stars, but are constantly bombarding the Earth, it is logical to argue that the building blocks of life, and indeed life itself, must have their origins viewed, according to the authors, from ".....a wider astronomical background".

Throughout his life, Fred Hoyle argued that nature does not separate the sciences into distinct and mutually exclusive disciplines in the way that academe does. The example of this notion given by the authors is the discovery in the eighteenth century of nebulae by Sir William Herschel and of the nucleus of living cells by Robert Brown. "The discoveries were made possible by advances in related experimental techniques - the construction of reflecting telescopes in one case and microscopes on the other....." yet over two centuries later we can see how these discoveries have resulted in an overlapping of the sciences of biology and astronomy. In their later work, "Diseases from Space", Hoyle and Wickramasinghe held that common cold and influenza viruses have their origin in comets and that these viruses and bacteria periodically enter the Earth's atmosphere. At the time, it was claimed that Hoyle and Wickramasinghe, not being qualified medical practitioners, were incapable of pronouncing on epidemiological issues. It is the opinion of the writer of this review that Hoyle and Wickramasinghe will soon be vindicated as the evidence of an extraterrestrial origin for viral and bacterial matter continues to mount. The day may not be too long off when we see the overlap of astronomy and medicine in a new discipline to be known perhaps as "astro-medicine".

The authors examine the birth of our solar system in the context of the chemistry of gas clouds and the origin of life. They reject the theory of the solar system's origins from a cooling gaseous protoplanet. If this had been the case then most of the Earth's mass would consist of water, neon and carbon rather than iron and rock. Instead, the authors argue that our present atmosphere and geological composition came at a later stage in the Earth's development and that the source of this composition was comets. Along with the materials that gave rise to the Earth's atmosphere and geology were pre-biotic molecules that eventually gave rise to life on the planet.

In the final two chapters of their book, Hoyle and Wickramasinghe examine the concept of life, and especially intelligent life, being prevalent on a galactic wide scale. They express their optimism that Earth is not the only life-bearing planet. The possibilities of space travel and colonisation of the galaxy by technologically capable species are given due consideration as is the feasibility of their being able to communicate with each other. One may argue that years of searching by those involved in the SETI project have so far yielded negative results and that this therefore must be discouraging for those who hold to the view that intelligent life has evolved on a galactic wide scale. Perhaps the directors of SETI would do well to read the final chapter of "Lifecloud" in which the authors propose a scanning system that dispenses with steerable dishes and instead adopts an alternative one that relies on fixed radio telescopes placed at regular intervals along a line of longitude. Such a strip of radio telescopic dishes could sweep the whole sky in just one or two days.

Although written thirty six years ago, this book is as up-to-date today as it was beyond its date when it first hit the bookshops. If any scientist of the current generation read this book and find that its sole influence is the realisation that breaking free from the straightjacket of scientific orthodoxy is the way that progress is made, then "Lifecloud", like all of Hoyle's and Wickramasinghe's works can still be considered as being highly worthwhile and extremely relevant to the twenty first century.

XIX

The Cosmogony of the Solar System:

by Fred Hoyle

The Cosmogony of the Solar System by Fred Hoyle is probably one of the best books which deals with the question of the origin of our solar system. It is somewhat technical in its details, but even the non-mathematical layman can, with perseverance, manage to get the gist of the work.

After finishing the Introduction which looks at one aspect of the scientific method regarding the discovery of laws using either few or many particles, the author goes on to consider the spin of the sun, a spin which was involved in the making of our solar system. Throughout the rest of the book, Hoyle looks at the chemical composition of the solar system and notes how the distribution of the elements throughout the system are related to its origins.

In Chapter 18, Hoyle takes a look at our nearest astronomical neighbour, the moon. He shows by reasoned argument that the dust on the lunar surface is not caused by lava flows as averred by the conventional theory, but rather by high energy electrons from the sun.

In the final chapter, Hoyle considers the issue of how life arose on Earth. He examines the close co-relation between the spectroscopic lines for cellulose in the laboratory and in astronomical objects such as the Trapezium Nebula. What Fred Hoyle briefly touches upon here, is more fully developed in his later works e.g. Diseases From Space where he transfers the entire theory of evolution to a much wider cosmic context.

XX

Diseases from Space:

by Fred Hoyle and N. C. Wickramasinghe

"Diseases from Space" by Fred Hoyle and Professor Chandra Wickramasinghe is rightly described by Sir Patrick Moore as "a revolutionary concept". This 244 page paperback is divided into 11 chapters, three appendices, a bibliography and an index. The core thesis of the work is the notion "..... that viruses and bacteria responsible for the infectious diseases of plants and animals arrive at the Earth from space". (chapter 1, page 1)

An idea of such highly contentious proportions would require evidential backing based upon both logical argument and meticulous research; and this is exactly what Hoyle and Wickramasinghe have done with the result that even those approaching this book with the highest possible degree of scepticism will be just that bit less sceptical by the time they have finished reading it.

The authors commence their work by arguing quite convincingly that life did not have its origins on the Earth itself due to the high oxygen content of the planet and the dangerous ultraviolet light emitted by the young sun - these, they point out, are highly detrimental to unstable organic molecules. However, conditions within comets are far more favourableto the development of organic molecules and viruses and bacteria. These were responsible for seeding the primeval Earth with life and with subsequently adding new genetic material for the evolution and development of new species throughout the eons. This process continues with the Earth receiving, on a regular basis, new viruses and bacteria which are responsible for influenza and common cold epidemics.

Perhaps the most controversial thing about this work is the authors' debunking of the most commonly accepted means by which influenza and colds are spread - person to person transmission. Their careful analyses of historical documentation together with their field work involving the gathering of information on the patterns of influenza infection among school children serve to seriously undermine the long and widely held view that viral and bacterial infections are spread like "buckets down a line". They clearly demonstrate that during the influenza pandemic of 1917 to 1919 large areas such as Alaska with low and widely dispersed populations were as much affected by the pandemic as regions of high population concentrations. The "patchiness" of influenza epidemics also tends to weaken the theory of person to person transmission. Perhaps the most convincing piece of evidence is in the astonishing finding that young people were infected with influenza during the times of the return of Halley's Comet whereas those aged 75 and above already had immunity.

Hoyle and Wickramasinghe point out that when medieval physicians spoke of "poisoned air" being the cause of plagues, we today fail to realise that they were nearer the mark than we tend to give them credit for. The authors show that killer diseases such as Bubonic Plague could not have been spread by the Black Rat on ships as the disease did not follow maritime routes and its occurrence was patchy rather than uniform. The rats, like people, died in the places where they were infected. The authors state that "....an overpowering edifice of scientific theory...." and"....scientific orthodoxy" have the effect today of stifling imagination and giving rise to "modern superstitions". (chapter 8 page 158)

The authors admit that to some, their ideas will appear to be "preposterous", however, they go on to state that "... in science one must steel oneself not to decide the correctness or otherwise of ideas according to subjective prejudices. In science, fact reigns supreme". (chapter 1 page 11) One of the major criticisms directed at the authors was that neither of them were qualified medical practitioners. In this regard it is worthwhile remembering what Hoyle once stated regarding the compartmentalisation of the sciences, to wit that nature does not work according to these artificial distinctions created by academia. If those involved in the various scientific disciplines could show more imagination and break free of their compartmentalised confinements greater progress could be made in all areas of research. Perhaps a new field known as "astro-medicine" could be opened up! Such a new area of medical research could greatly enhance the prediction and treatment of diseases and how the medical profession responds to these epidemics. Those who have dismissed

Hoyle's and Wickramasinghe's ideas out of hand are surely acting less than professionally. To say that their theory of diseases originating in space is "fantasy" without first taking cognizance of their evidence and mode of reasoning is in itself a fantasy!

XXI

Common Sense in Nuclear Energy:

by Fred Hoyle and Geoffrey Hoyle

Like its predecessor "Energy or Extinction - The Case for Nuclear Energy", "Commonsense in Nuclear Energy" clearly sets out the case for the urgency of the adoption of nuclear energy as an alternative to the rapidly dwindling supplies of hydrocarbons. At the time of writing this review, the British Prime Minister, Mr. Gordon Brown, has announced that seven new nuclear power plants are to be constructed in Great Britain. Welcome though this decision is, it still falls very far short of the 200 nuclear power plants that the authors of "Commonsense in Nuclear Energy" advise is needed if the nation is to obtain all its energy from nuclear power. President George Bush of the United States of America has recommended the stepping up of the search for the discovery of new oil fields, but this merely postpones the inevitable, it does not solve the long-term energy problem, for oil, like all fossil fuels, is a finite resource.

"Commonsense in Nuclear Energy" is an 85 page book co-authored by Fred Hoyle and his son Mr. Geoffrey Hoyle. It is published by W.H. Freeman and Company and consists of a preface, 16 chapters and an index. Although it came out in 1980, the issues it raises with regard to nuclear power are as relevant today as they were then. That the anti-nuclear lobby is expressing the same concerns and misgivings about nuclear energy as it did back in the '70's and '80's, goes to clearly show that nothing has changed and little has been done to educate the public with regard to the true nature of nuclear energy. As this book debunks myth after myth about nuclear power, one cannot help but be convinced that if it were widely read today, a more enlightened consensus among the general public would serve to ensure that Britain's plans for nuclear power would be much further advanced than they currently are.

In their preface, the authors make a clear distinction between nuclear power and nuclear war. They contend that an energy shortage caused by population increase and diminishing supplies of hydrocarbons would be a sure recipe for conflict. Therefore, the implementation of policies designed to wean the world away from the fossil fuels of coal and oil would be the best bet for ensuring that the global stockpile of nuclear weapons would not be unleashed.

The authors take great pains to point out that they are both ardent conservationists. One of the myths which they successfully explode is the one which contends that nuclear energy is harmful to the environment. They explain how hydroelectric schemes are extremely detrimental to the environment. The raising and lowering of the water levels of natural lakes has had a deleterious effect on the flora which have followed the seasonal fluctuations of the water levels of the lakes. This, together with the visual pollution of unsightly dams has, as the authors explain, added very little to meeting the country's energy requirements.

The main thesis of this book is that the nuclear industry is one of the safest of all. The authors explain that, contrary to popular misconceptions, nuclear power stations do not explode and they go on to demonstrate that gas cylinders and various chemicals have far greater explosive potential than nuclear power plants. One of the most amusing things they point out is that there are the same ingredients in a bar of chocolate as in TNT, yet no-one would dream of banning chocolate on the grounds that it is a combustible hazard! When it comes to deaths through industrial accidents, the nuclear industry comes out smelling of roses, as there are more hazards in coal and oil exploration than there are in the production of nuclear energy. The authors show that statistically we have a much greater chance of meeting our end in car and plane accidents and from natural disasters than we do from nuclear accidents. When it comes to exposure to radiation, it is found that there is vastly more radiation from our natural surroundings than from nuclear power plants. The bar graph on page 20 indicates that of all the sources of radioactivity, the lowest of all is to be found in the production of nuclear power.

The authors examine non-nuclear options as an alternative to hydrocarbons and conclude that they are not viable propositions. They explain that deep drilling for natural gas could result in earthquakes. Solar, wind and wave power are ruled out due to the massive engineering constructions that would be necessary in order to successfully concentrate and distribute the energy derived from them. The authors explain the cardinal rule which underlies the entire energy debate, which rule being that energy derived from any source must be more than the energy expended in obtaining it.

Another myth which the authors successfully demolish is the one which claims that the storage of nuclear waste presents an environmental hazard. Calculations undertaken by the American Physical Society indicate that nuclear waste buried 3,000 feet underground would take over one million years to percolate to the surface.

The authors' conclusion is that the most efficient type of nuclear technology is the fast breeder reactor. When commenting on the fears of this form of nuclear production, they devote their final chapter to a comparison between the forebodings of the anti steam engine groups about George Stephenson's locomotive and railways on the one hand and those of the anti-nuclear lobby on the other. This comparison serves to put the whole nuclear issue in a proper and rational perspective. After reading this book, one cannot help but feel that society must conquer its fears about nuclear energy and overcome its lingering Luddite mentality if the horrors of an energy crisis are to be averted.

XXII

The Origin of Life:

by Fred Hoyle and N. C. Wickramasinghe

For those who wish to embark upon an in-depth study of astrobiology by reading the works on this theory by its chief protagonists, Fred Hoyle and Nadine Chandra Wickramasinghe, and who would consider some kind of general framework as constituting a beneficial starting point for their studies, they would do well to begin with this 15 page pamphlet "The Origin of Life," as it provides a very helpful synoptic overview of what astrobiology is and what its implications are for medicine, evolution and the origin of life itself.

The core thesis in the Hoyle/Wickramasingheastrobiological theory is that the origin of life is transferred from being the construct of a purely terrestrial phenomenon to one which involves the resources of the entire cosmos both in terms of time and material. In highlighting the improbabilities of life's starting point being the Earth, the authors point out the complexity of the initial life forms which were present on the planet a little over half a billion years after its birth. Bacteria brought to Earth by comets, meteorites and other astronomical bodies merely required of terrestrial evolutionary biology ".....an unraveling of a wide range of cosmically determined possibilities" (P. 7).

That the genetic input driving the engine of evolution involves a mechanism whereby space based bacteria is deposited on the Earth, is a theory which is rendered added impetus by the authors' historical analyses of the incidences of epidemic diseases which clearly depict their entrances onto and exits from the stage of human medical experience at widely divergent intervals consisting of hundreds of years. A close study of epidemiological periods indicates a rapidity of spread which defies explanation by the widely accepted conventional human to human transmission mechanism. Spectroscopic studies which have examined the absorption and emission lines of gas clouds and dust in the interstellar medium, indicate a dovetailing with those conducted on laboratory bacteria.

In this short booklet, Hoyle and Wickramasinghe have put together a highly convincing case for the "deprecopernicanisation" of life. In their more detailed compositions, these two highly distinguished scientists flesh out the evidence to support their theory, a theory which involves nothing less than a paradigm shift in the way the biological sciences are both presented and conducted.

XXIII

The Relation of Biology to Astronomy:

by Fred Hoyle

"The Relation of Biology to Astronomy" is a small pamphlet type publication based upon a lecture delivered by the author, Fred Hoyle, in 1980. The issue about which the lecture is concerned is the nature of interstellar dust. Hoyle began his lecture by explaining the effect this dust has upon starlight, vis, that it causes it to fog - the technical term being `extinction.'

The next part of the lecture was concerned with the nature of this interstellar dust - the basic question being as to what it actually is. A decade previously, Hoyle and his colleague, Chandra Wickramasinghe, had predicted that a peak in the extinction of a wavelength of 2,200A for graphite soot particles would be found. While this peak was in fact found, graphite particles could not be held to account for the extinction on either of its side as "On the ultraviolet side, the extinction is caused mainly by a scattering of radiation, whereas graphite causes extinction mainly by absorption." Hoyle then went on to give a number of other reasons as to why graphite could not be the cause of the extinction - for example, that on the visual side, it is too high for graphite.

Hoyle demonstrated that other candidates such as MgSiO3 and MgO, SiO and SiO2 to explain the composition of the dust were not possible given interstellar conditions. It was at this point in the lecture that Hoyle turned to biology as a viable theory to explain the phenomenon of interstellar dust. It is cellulose rather than graphite which more readily accounts for the extinction at 2,200A in the ultraviolet part of the spectrum. Hoyle then made his most astonishing - nay, revolutionary - statement that interstellar grains are in fact bacteria! This was no wild speculation as the extinction curves obtained in the laboratory for bacteria matched those obtained by observation.

More than 30 years after the time this lecture was delivered, much work still needs to be done in order to establish once and for all the biological basis for interstellar dust. This is mainly due to hostility on the part of the mainstream scientific establishment which, almost in blinkered fashion, refuses to even investigate the issue with any due consideration. We can only hope for a change in attitude!

XXIV

Steady State Cosmology Revisited:

by Fred Hoyle

In "Steady-State Cosmology Re-Visited", Fred Hoyle admits that after the discovery in 1965 of the microwave background radiation, his faith in what is essentially his own theory regarding the origins of the Universe had waned somewhat. The re-examination of the Steady State Theory within the light of the 1965 and other discoveries in the field of cosmology, served to put this interpretation of cosmic origins back on track as an alternative to the Big Bang Theory. "Steady-State Cosmology Re-visited" encapsulates this new-found confidence wrought by a more careful consideration of the cosmological phenomena which astronomers and astrophysicists began to study in the 1960's and '70's.

After rendering a general historical background and overview of the Steady-State model, Hoyle goes on to explain that the corrections applied to the red-shift magnitude curve for galaxies brings this curve more into line with the SS theory.

The author then goes on to show that the distribution of radio sources, according to the counting procedure practiced by Sir Martin Ryle, was pitted with errors. Subsequent corrections brought the slope of magnitude back to the 1.5 figure associated with a Steady State Universe.

It is with regard to the apparent coup de grace given to Steady-State Cosmology by the discovery of the microwave background radiation that Hoyle's alternative explanations give renewed credence to his Bondi's and Gold's cosmological model. Hoyle explains the uniformity of the background microwave radiation in terms of "white holes" and graphite particles. When material streams out of a white hole, a process known as "decoupling" occurs whereby matter and radiation are separated. It is the emergence of this material from the white holes and the decoupling process which accounts for the microwave radiation.

In Part II of this book, Hoyle links his SS cosmological model to the question of life and how it relates to the wider cosmos. He examines the mathematical improbability of life arising by mere chance and so places evolution in a wider cosmic context noting that the MeV positionings for the Carbon and Oxygen atom are not accidental phenomena but linked to the ability of the Universe to produce life.

"Steady-State Cosmology Re-visited"was written in 1980, and in 2012 (the year of writing this review), the astronomical community still adheres tenaciously to the Big Bang Model. Perhaps, a "re-visiting" to this book may result in a long-overdue tilt being made more in favour of the Steady State Theory!

XXV

ICE:

by Fred Hoyle

"Ice - The Ultimate Human Catastrophe" shows its author, Fred Hoyle, at his scientific best. The book is extremely well researched and its core arguments are backed up with tables, diagrams, maps and photographs. The technical notes at the back of the book give further substance to the various scientific processes discussed in the main body of the work.

In his Introduction, Fred Hoyle relates how his interest in the various ice ages of the Earth started during his days as a postgraduate research student at Cambridge. In the 1930's, the numbers of students involved in research were very small and this fact provided the chance for students to debate quite freely issues concerning each other's disciplines. It was no doubt this openness in an era of not too deep and restricted specialisation that gave Hoyle the versatility of mind to write on a variety of issues outside of his field of mathematics and astronomy. In fact, in this book, Hoyle successfully contradicts some of the theories of those who specialise in the Earth sciences when the causes of global cooling are being examined.

In the first of the eleven chapters of which this book is composed, Hoyle excites the imagination by vividly describing what the ice age world must not only have looked like, but indeed felt like. One can almost feel oneself starting to shiver from the icy blast! The second chapter describes the positive impact the last ice age would have had on the human species. As mankind would have had to compete with large and powerful animals for the scarce food resources available, a surge in the development of hunting methods and technology occurred in order for the human species to survive this tremendous challenge posed by nature.

Hoyle then goes on to examine the controversy which ensued in the 18th and 19th centuries regarding ice ages and how the scientific community at the time came round to accepting that there must indeed have been times when the glaciers extended much further than their present day limits. He explains that the widespread distribution of boulders from their source of origin was ample evidence of an ice age.

After establishing the clear and convincing evidence for past ice ages, the book then deals with the causes of these cold epochs in the Earth's geological history. The variations in the Earth's axis of rotation as calculated by Croll and Milankovitch cause too slight a temperature variation to be a means by which the planet could undergo such vast cooling. Having given due consideration to biological, volcanic, cyclonic and glacier slippage theories as explanations for the Earth's cooling, Hoyle logically demonstrates that ice ages are brought on by large meteorites impacting with the Earth. Meteorites with a force large enough to throw up reflective dust high into the atmosphere and so block out the sun occur around every 100,000 years or so, and Hoyle gives us the chilling warning that we are due for another such collision (and thus another ice age) quite soon. In the concluding chapter of his work, Hoyle describes the sort of advanced engineering project which could and should be undertaken to prevent another catastrophic ice age. Pumping up cold water from the depths of the ocean to be heated nearer the surface would increase latent oceanic heat, enough to feed the land (the heat sink) until the reflective particles thrown up by the meteorite fell from the stratosphere to the land.

At a time when we hear so much about global warming, this book provides a healthy balance to the current climate debate. We come to understand from its pages that the planet on which we live is more prone to extreme cold than to extreme heat and that the present warm spell we are now going through and which we may be erroneously terming as "global warming" may well indeed be nothing more than a brief inter-glacial period.

XXVI

The Physics-Astronomy Frontier:

by Fred Hoyle & Jayant Narlikar

"The Physics-Astronomy Frontier," authored by Fred Hoyle and Professor Jayant V. Narlikar, is, as its title suggests, a work which unites the disciplines of Physics and Astronomy. This well-illustrated book is divided into three parts, each of which examines the various aspects of Astronomy and Physics - or, as we might say - Astrophysics.

The first section of this work deals with the electrical interaction and looks at radiation, quantum mechanics and spectrum lines. The authors show that the issue of radiation cannot be studied as a phenomenon separate from particles, but rather, that the radiative interaction of one particle can have an effect on another. The authors treat on the various different forms of astronomy such as radio, millimeter-wave and x-ray astronomy and explain their specific uses in studying different forms of astronomical phenomena.

The second part of the book explores the micro world of atomic nuclei within the context of stellar formation. The authors describe how stars generate energy by means of nuclear fusion processes and their manner of evolution from their birth in large gaseous nebulae to their deaths either as black holes or white dwarves.

In the third part of the book, Hoyle and Narlikar consider the mysterious physics related to black holes and how these strange objects are detected. This section of the work also looks at the wider cosmological perspective and discusses the various models devised to explain the origin of the Universe.

Although this book may be somewhat technical for the average lay reader, it does provide a wealth of material for the Physics student who may be contemplating a career in the astrophysical sciences. It clearly demonstrates the inter-relatedness of two subjects, each of which are, to a great extent, dependent upon the other.

XXVII

Evolution from Space:

by Fred Hoyle & N. C. Wickramasinghe

Evolution From Space by Fred Hoyle and N. Chandra Wickramasinghe is a ground-breaking work which surely serves to cast doubt on Darwinian evolution and cause biologists to look afresh at life's origins. Every chapter is full of surprises. Why do we find globin genes in legumes? Why are bacteria able to survive in conditions which are not found on Earth? And why do flies see at wavelengths of 2,537 Angstrom - a wavelength which does not exist naturally on Earth? The answer to this question is one of the biggest surprises in the book - insects come from outer space. The authors argue that there is simply no selective pressure for insects and microorganisms to evolve these adaptive properties on Earth, so an extraterrestrial environment for the selective pressure factors must logically be considered.

Hoyle and Wickramasinghe demonstrate the mathematical impossibility of amino acids in a single gene rearranging themselves to become functional within a Darwinain evolutionary timescale.

Their way of explaining the absence of intermediate species in the fossil record (an awkward fact for Darwinian evolution which insists on a gradual process involving intermediate species) is also quite novel. Evolution per saltum(by a jump) is caused by fresh inputs of cosmic genes which rain down on the Earth and which are acquired by species best able to use them.

Unlike so many scientists, Hoyle and Wickramasinghe do not dodge the fundamental question of the Universe (and life in particular) being controlled by some form of Intelligence - or God. In the final chapter, the authors postulate a theory which involves a sequence of Intelligences: one which "...designed the bio-chemicals and gave rise to the origin of carbonaceous life". Another higher level of Intelligence was responsible for controlling "...the coupling constants of physics." And how many of these Intelligences are there? "But like a convergent mathematical sequence of functions it has an idealised limit.....it is this idealised limit that is God...." And the authors' final conclusion is that God is the Universe.

XXVIII

The Quasar Controversy Resolved:

by Fred Hoyle

Quasars were first discovered by three radio-astronomers (Hanbury Brown, Allen and Palmer) at Jodrell Bank in 1961. At the time of writing (2012), controversy still rages regarding their distances, and distance was the core issue which Fred Hoyle attempted to tackle in his book The Quasar Controversy Resolved.

Hoyle begins by examining the three main causes for the spectroscopic red shift found in astronomical phenomena: the expansion of the universe; the Doppler affect which occurs when bodies move away from us; and, light which emerges from a strong gravitational field and moves to a weaker gravitational field. Astronomers generally reject the third of these alternatives as the absorption lines "....are too narrow to permit strong gravitation....". The second explanation, Hoyle explains, is rejected on the grounds that if quasars could be explained in term of the Doppler shift, then it would stand to reason that the motions of some of these objects would indicate movement towards as well as away from us thus producing a blue shift in the former case. What Hoyle calls "the conformist position" accepts the first explanation as the one which accounts for the large red shift found in quasars. Yet, it is this very "conformist position" which Hoyle rejects. He suggests that either the Doppler affect be examined more closely, or else, some unknown and complex form of physics is involved in producing the red shifts of quasars.

A great part of the book is devoted to a description of the dramatis personae and the events involved in tackling the issue of quasars. This provides an insight into the `politics' which so often bedevils science - the allocation of funds, use of equipment and so forth.

Since the publication of this book in 1980, much has been discovered about the nature of quasars but the controversy regarding their distances remains in spite of the "conformist" position still being highly entrenched. However, any astrophysicist who would feel so inclined to embark upon a more critical evaluation of the consensus regarding the cosmological distances of quasars, would do well to look at Hoyle's reasoning as it is displayed in the book and particularly at the more technical analysis of the issue given jointly in an appendix with Prof. JayantNarlikar.

XXIX

Space Travellers:

by Fred Hoyle & Chandra Wickramasinghe

"Space Travellers: The Bringers of Life", written by Fred Hoyle and Prof. Chandra Wickramasinghe, and published in 1981 contains 13 chapters and a technical appendage. Following hot on the heels of its predecessor, "Diseases from Space," this book continues the great saga of its far-sighted authors in their attempts to convince the somewhat staid scientific community of a completely different approach being required to explain the origins and transmission of many common diseases such as influenza, the cold and smallpox.

While there is a considerable amount of overlap with both its predecessor (vide supra) and its successors of similar genre, "Space Travellers: The Bringers of Life" being dedicated to the memory of Svante Arrhenius, takes the path of tracing the historical origins of the theory of life as a cosmic rather than as merely a terrestrial phenomenon. Hoyle and Wickramasinghe start with the theory as advocated by Arrhenius (that bacteria may travel from one planet to another) and modify and develop it according to the latest research on the subject.

By demonstrating that viruses and bacteria are well adapted to withstand the hazards of radiation in space and that given certain precautions may survive the perilous journey down through the Earth's atmosphere, the authors successfully overcome the objections put in the way by critics of the theory. They then convincingly argue the case for comets being the principle mechanism whereby viral and bacterial substances are delivered to planetary bodies.

The ingenious manner by which Hoyle and Wickramasinghe bolster their theory of viruses and bacteria being incident from space is by a consideration of the spread of common diseases on Earth. On a thorough examination of the medical records from periods of influenza outbreak, the two scientists show by means of their research into the patterns of infectionin institutions where communal living exists (boarding schools, for example) that the theory of person to person transmission, in all its essentials, completely breaks down. The simultaneous outbreak of influenza in widely separated places prior to the advent of air-travel, and people, such as shepherds, living in isolation from any human contact, yet succumbing to the disease, were phenomena also used by Hoyle and Wickramasinghe to argue against the horizontal spread (i.e. human to human) of influenza.

While those perusing this book without any familiarity with its predecessors and successors will surely find its pages full of surprises, there can be little doubt that the biggest surprise, nay, utter shock! is reserved for the final chapter, interrogatively entitled "Biology or Astronomy?" in which the two authors convincingly argue the case for the structural and functioning order of the Universe being driven by essentially biological forces in the form of bacteria. Hoyle and Wickramasinghe conclude their work by pondering on whether the threat lies in biology being swallowed up into astronomy or astronomy being swallowed up into biology. In the wider consideration of Fred Hoyle's philosophy of intricate inter-linkage among all the academic disciplines, it may be a reasonable conclusion that astronomy and biology are in the process of being merged into a discipline which sees the Universe anew as a territory tantalisingly awaiting the application of new tools and new ideas for the revelation of its many secrets. In the wonderment as to whether or not the Universe will yield up those secrets, there is surely an awareness that the Cosmos' co-operation in thisis highly dependent upon those engaged in the pursuit of science opening up the vehicles of their own minds and mustering up the courage for what can most undoubtedly be described as the reward of an exciting journey lying ahead of them.

XXX

The Anglo-Australian Telescope:

by Fred Hoyle

"The Anglo-Australian Telescope" by Fred Hoyle is an interesting 27 page booklet which meticulously walks us through the procedures leading up to the construction and completion of a joint venture between Britain and Australia in the field of astronomical research. Hoyle states, "I know of no more beautiful setting of a telescope anywhere in the world" (p.24) and " - ….the AAT is certainly among the best two or three telescopes in the world " (p.26), and, "the AAT is not infrequently spoken of as the best in the world" (p.26); yet the bureaucratic and administrative agonising that went into the making of this telescope a success surely belies the aesthetic qualities inherent in the instrument's design and location.

From the commencement of proceedings in 1965 to inauguration in 1974, the tale of the telescope is a labyrinthine tangle of problems related to bureaucracy, contract tenders, technical issues and design. What perhaps makes this instrument more astonishing than its combination of pleasing aesthetics coupled with technical excellence, is that Hoyle, along with some other big guns in the astronomical world (Redman, Lovell, Bruck and Ryle) favoured an alternative project for a telescope located in the Mediterranean rather than in Australia (p.5), and, that the eventual design of the instrument varied so much from the original Kit Peak template that many astronomers predicted that the eventual outcome would be a "disaster" (p.26).

Can this small booklet have any relevance in the first two decades of the twenty-first century? Perhaps the most remarkable outcome of this drama is that in spite of the tremendous obstacles placed in the paths of both the individual and corporate dramatis personae was that the telescope project turned out to be a resounding success. By taking note of the various bureaucratic, technical and contractual hurdles placed in the paths of those involved with the AAT project, organisations such as the Scientific Research Council (SRC), the Department of Education and Science (DES), and the Royal Society (RS) can plan a smoother administrative path and an easier bureaucratic process when venturing upon the construction of scientific instruments.

XXXI

Facts and Dogmas in Cosmology and Elsewhere:

by Fred Hoyle

Robert Rede, who was appointed Chief Justice of the Common Please in 1506, founded three public lectureships in Cambridge. These were reorganised into a single lecture in 1859, and in 1982, Fred Hoyle, as the Rede Lecturer for that year, delivered "Facts and Dogmas in Cosmology and Elsewhere" as the title of his address.

Hoyle's description of his favourite walk in what was then his home in the Lake District was no inapt opening to his talk, as the activity he found to be most conducive to the mulling over in his mind the issues of great moment, was in traversing landscapes off the beaten track, wild and rugged in their topography.

Hoyle had consistently averred that while the distinctions drawn by academe between the various scientific disciplines were purely artificial, nature recognised no such divisions. It is against this backdrop of academic interconnectedness that Hoyle's reminiscences into his childhood years permits of diligent observation the discernment of what is clearly the enigma of the young Fred Hoyle, unenthusiastic about Christianity, yet, to the profound consternation of his school-mate contemporaries, topping the religious education exams, and the Fred Hoyle of later years demonstrating by the scientific empirical method the overwhelming evidence that some form of Intelligence is responsible for the intricate and detailed structure clearly evident in the Universe.

Though Hoyle employed the analogy of the extreme unlikelihood of three billiard balls meeting simultaneously on the same part of the table as justification of his rejection of an explanation of the cosmos which involves the notions of 'chance' and 'accident', the three 'billiard balls' of astronomy, biology and theology, in astonishing fashion do precisely that on the billiard table of the Rede Lecture!

XXXII

The Intelligent Universse:

by Fred Hoyle

In "The Intelligent Universe", Fred Hoyle takes his idea of Panspermia theory to a higher level and asks what is perhaps the most fundamental question of all to humanity - who or what is God? While most of mainstream science wants nothing to do with these sort of philosophical questions, Hoyle does not duck the issue, but instead clearly demonstrates that sooner or later scientists will have to face up to the notion of some form of higher intelligence controlling the Universe.

In the first chapter, Hoyle shows that, mathematically speaking, it is impossible for life to have been formed on Earth by mere random chance. He further points out that "....even the most complex viruses..... are nevertheless unable to reproduce themselves in any form of non-living organic soup". Chapter 2 is mainly devoted to showing how Darwinian evolution is wrong namely in that the fossil record shows evolution by major leaps rather than by slow degrees involving minor changes producing intermediate forms. Hoyle goes on to demonstrate in chapter 3 that there is abundant evidence that life in viral and bacterial form exist outside the Earth in comets, meteorites and asteroids. In the following chapter the author considers the evidence which suggests that interstellar dust is in fact bacterial, and in chapter 5 he takes this one step further by arguing that it is fresh input of cosmic genetic material from cometary sources which produces the main source and channel for evolution. As in his previous publications, Hoyle here repeats his claim that many supposedly infectious diseases originate in outer space and links these diseases with the process of evolution - diseases thus being resultant from a genetic mismatch of the DNA of the incoming pathogen with that of the host organism onto which it falls. Hoyle devotes most of Chapter 6 to dismissing the popular idea of UFOs.

He clearly explains why interstellar space travel can never be a viable option, but goes on to develop the concept of life's unity arising from its pervasion throughout the cosmos rather than the more generally accepted view of its confinement to isolated planets in isolated solar systems. Chapter 7 is extremely interesting in its controversial re-interpretation of the cosmic background microwave radiation. Hoyle dismisses the popular interpretation of the phenomenon as being the result of the Big Bang and instead avers that the radiation is caused by bacteria enclosed within long whiskers of carbon. In this way, Hoyle unites the concept of life's cosmic origins with that of the Steady State Theory. In Quantum mechanics, radiation flows in a past to future time-frame; as Hoyle explains in Chapter 8, this leads to "...degeneration, to senescence, to the loss of information." In grappling to account for the opposite effect in biology where organisms increase in sophistication and complexity, Hoyle suggests a situation in which radiation runs in an opposite time-frame which is from future to past. This leads on to the question as to what intelligence is up to. In Chapter 9 Hoyle answers this question by suggesting that the intelligence which is controlling the Universe is constantly adapting life to changing circumstances which may lead to the end of carbon based life at some distant point in the future. He espouses the hypothesis that the exceptional talents found in certain "gifted" individuals such as Shakespeare, Einstein or Mozart may be the result of fresh genetic input from cosmic viruses arriving on the Earth. Hoyle states that these abilities go way beyond the immediate needs of day to day survival within a context of natural selection. He goes on to suggest that these individuals of exceptional abilities "....are markers on the path along which our species appear destined to tread." In the final chapter of this book, Hoyle contends that the human drive to "...enquire into matters ....far removed from daily life..." is part and parcel of the pre-programming in humans to reach outwards towards the ultimate intelligence which controls the Universe, an intelligence from which all life had its origin and with which we need to get closer to if humanity is to survive.

"The Intelligent Universe" is a highly readable book for both the qualified scientist and the layman. It is most unlikely that anyone will read this book without coming away quite a different person; without becoming someone who is more aware of their connections to the wider cosmos and humanity's place within it.

XXXIII

From Grains to Bacteria:

by Fred Hoyle and Chandra Wickramasinghe

Although since the publication of "From Grains to Bacteria" in 1984, the existence of organic substances in interstellar gas clouds has assumed the status of standard accepted fact, the scientific community still has not come round even to a reasonable consideration that interstellar dust may in fact be of a bacterial composition.

As the co-authors of this book, Fred Hoyle and N. Chandra Wickramasinghe, make clear that their initial research into the nature and composition of interstellar dust was carried out within a framework involving conventional models and orthodox theory, and that accumulating observational data, particularly in the form of spectroscopy, failed to fit these standard models, it would surely not be in breach of any code of scientific procedure wherein is involved an objective and empirical analyses of the data, to examine more closely the microbial explanation as a substitute for the failing orthodox models regarding interstellar dust.

That Hoyle and Wickramasinghe did not arrive lightly at the conclusion that interstellar dust is essentially microbial, is well attested to by the historical format in which these authors lay out the chronology of events leading up to their unconventional yet bold assertion that interstellar dust is composed of desiccated bacteria.

The presentation of the evidence in such a clear and detailed manner must surely leave the reader who cares to study this work from cover to cover with the sincere hope that the eschewing of this more satisfactory explanation for interstellar grains will soon be abandoned by the mainstream scientific community.

XXXIV

Living Comets:

by Fred Hoyle and Chandra Wickramasinghe

"Living Comets", written by Fred Hoyle and Professor Nadine Chandra Wickramasinghe, follows the theme of the many other publications of these two authors (such as "Diseases from Space" and "Life on Mars") in which they take the origins of life and its evolutionary processes out of their narrow terrestrial context and place them within a wider cosmological framework.

The highly technical nature of the book should not be an off-putting factor for the lay reader, as perseverance with its contents will reap the reward of gleaning much of its underlying thesis – namely that life was transported to Earth via comets and that the beginnings of biology are not to be looked for on planetary bodies but in the Oort Cloud surrounding the solar system.

Before considering the chemical and possible biological aspects of cometary bodies, the authors begin their work by examining Halley's Comet within its historical framework, mainly from the time Sir Edmund Halley calculated its orbit and thus its 75 year periodical visits to the Earth's orbital plane.

After treating on the issue of cometary orbits, the authors then attempt to place these objects within a wider galactic context. By mathematical calculation, they show how passing stars can push comets from the Oort Cloud into the inner regions of the solar system thus replenishing short-lived comets which generally end their lives between the orbits of Mars and Jupiter.

It is about half way through the book that Hoyle and Wickramasinghe deal with the possible biological nature of comets and how they are pivotal in bringing viral and bacterial life to the inner solar system. The two authors once again aver that so-called infectious diseases are incident from space. They see these diseases as part and parcel of the wider evolutionary processes whereby new DNA is brought to the Earth and that some of this new genetic material will be beneficial to terrestrial organisms for the enhancement of their ability to adapt, by means of Natural Selection, to changing environmental conditions. Itis somewhat ironical that this book is currently out of print. Thoughit was written in 1985, it is only in more recent years that the greaterscientific community is beginning to take more seriously the distinctpossibility that life is a cosmological phenomenon and that its genesisis to be found in space rather than on planetary bodies.

XXXV

The Origin of the Universe and the Origin of Religion:

by Fred Hoyle

"The Origin of the Universe and the Origin of Religion" was the subject of a lecture delivered by Fred Hoyle, circa 1993, at the AnshemTransdisciplinary Lectureships in Art, Science and the Philosophy of Culture. The book by the same title is essentially a transcript of this, the second lecture, in the Lectureship series.

In the first of the five sections into which Hoyle divided the transcript of his lecture, the issue of certainty and uncertainty in matters scientific within a context of what is generally deemed "respectability," is dealt with by Hoyle arguing that the vast areas of knowledge upon which scientists agree because of their workability in the realm of technology constitute the "certainty" aspect of science. In the areas of uncertainty, where scientific opinions differ markedly, Hoyle contends that the scientific consensus will undoubtedly be incorrect owing to the persistence of the problems in defying solutions for considerable periods of time. Using the theories concerning the origin of the universe and the origin of life as examples, Hoyle demonstrates that it is in operating within the parameters laid down by conventional modes of thinking that scientists gain "respectability" in their profession

It is in the second part of the lecture, entitled "Ice Ages and Comets" that Hoyle proceeds to show how his own thinking outside of the box is "disrespectful" by its unconventionality. Hoyle begins by explaining how the examination of species of beetle remains in mud layers is indicative of temperatures on Earth in the northern latitudes 13,000 years ago - different beetle species being able to survive within very narrow temperature variations. After considering the theories concerning the reasons for the onset of an ice age, and concluding that they ensue from the combination of a dry atmosphere causing volcanic ash spewed up into the atmosphere to form into ice crystals which increase solar reflectivity back into outer space, Hoyle turns his main focus on the processes by which ice ages come to a termination. As volcanic activity would be insufficient to melt the ice crystals, Hoyle argues for cometary impact as being the necessary means of warming the oceans and jettisoning the required 100 million tons of water into the atmosphere. It is this explanation of how ice ages come to an end that constitutes Hoyle's starting point in providing examples of how astronomical bodies impacting the Earth have been the causative agent in the major epochs of human development and progress. Hoyle convincingly argues that repeated impacts from cometary fragments would have produced a kind of "natural smelting" and thus have taught man the methods of obtaining metal from stone. It was the discovery of metal and charcoal by means of meteoric impact that mankind emerged from the Stone Age into the Iron Age.

Based upon the Clube and Napier hypothesis of the break-up of a giant comet 13,000 years ago, Hoyle, in the section entitled "The General Situation in Post-Ice Age Times," calculated the rate of impact according to cometary fragment sizes. Given the comet's original orbit, Hoyle contended that major bombardments would occur every 1,600 years. The extinction of the mammoths, the apparent motionless of the sun as witnessed by Joshua and the unexpected victory of the Saxons over the Vikings at Brunnenburgh, are all explained by Hoyle in terms of cometary fragment impact profoundly affecting the Earth's environment.

The part of the lecture under the title of "Comets and the Origin of Religions," Hoyle attributed the phenomena of "the bolts and lightnings of Zeus" of Classical times to the brilliant and colourful displays of cometary pieces burning up on impact with the Earth's atmosphere. From these atmospheric displays would develop the notion of wars between the gods. Hoyle also attributes the pyramidal shape of the most famous structures of ancient Egypt as being designed to withstand meteoric impact. Even the demise of the Roman Empire is explained in terms of a violent meteoric impact that shook the cities of Constantinople and Rome.

Hoyle, interestingly enough, takes an unconventionally positive stance towards the historical period known as the Dark Ages. He relates in his final section "Emergence into Medieval and Modern Times," how inventiveness increased during this era due to a concentration upon localised community and individual needs. Ironically however, according to Hoyle, the doctrinal mantle of the Earth being unaffected by anything outside of itself, has fallen upon modern day science. As Sir Isaac Newton felt uncomfortable with the notion of Earth-crossing comets having terrestrial consequences, so $20^{th}/21^{st}$ century science tends to eschew extraterrestrial phenomena as a means of affecting change on our planet. It is the same "respectability" that Hoyle so berated at the commencement of his lecture. At the close of the lecture, Hoyle contended that within a purely terrestrial context, physics has gone about as far as it can go, and if it is to progress any further it will need to be elevated onto a wider cosmic level. This concept of cosmological dimensionality can quite logically be extended to other areas of scientific discipline.

XXXVI

Viruses from Space:

by Fred Hoyle, Chandra Wickramasinghe and John Watkins

"Viruses from Space" by Fred Hoyle, Chandra Wickramasinghe and John Watkins, presents in its eight chapters, highly convincing evidence that many common diseases such as the cold, influenza, smallpox and whooping cough have their origins in outer space and that person-to-person transmission (horizontal transmission) is false. This book is essentially a follow on from "Diseases from Space" (Hoyle&Wickramasinghe) published in 1979 when the controversial theory of viruses incident from space was first mooted.

In the first chapter, the three authors make the pointed statement that horizontal transmission of diseases "....appears to have arisen through historical accident rather than through accurate observation and experiment (P.1)." One of the reasons given by Hoyle, Wickramasinghe and Watkins for resistance to an alternative to the person-to-person hypothesis in pathogenic transmission is the stubbornness inherent in the system which rejects any evidence which militates against established false belief.

Chapter three of the book examines the outbreak of acute upper respiratory disease which occurred during a conference in Sri Lanka in 1982 at which two of the authors (FH& CW) attended. Many of the conference participants were infected, including the two authors, and it was generally assumed that the disease had been brought by an astronomer from New York who had come to attend the conference. However, it was discovered on investigation by Hoyle and Wickramasinghe that while many of the conference participants were infected, their spouses and families were not. By examining the attack rates in schools in the vicinity of the hotel where most participants were put up and the conference hall, and the dispensation of medicines from a reputable Colombo chemist, the two authors concluded in favour of a vertical rather than a horizontal transmission process for the disease.

By bringing an historical perspective into their work, the authors turned their attention to investigating the plague at Athens in the year 430BC, the essential question under consideration being – "was it smallpox?" Their final analysis was that while the plague cannot be definitely identified as having been that of smallpox, the latter is a convincing enough candidate for being the disease which struck the city.

The sixth chapter takes the issue of cosmic pathogens into a most fascinating evolutionary dimension where the authors, by examining the effects incoming viroids have on the DNA in a plant or animal genome, aver that these viroids spur on the processes of biological change and adaptation. While most of the DNA in a genome is genetically unexpressed, an incoming viroid may be able to lock onto a portion of DNA and activate a hitherto dormant gene – haemoglobin in diseased legumes being the specific example of this given by the authors (p. 60).

The authors, in the fifth, seventh and eighth chapters of their book, clearly demonstrate by examining the distribution of influenza attack rates in boarding schools, the invalidity of the horizontal transmission hypothesis. It was essentially the random nature of infections that served to convince the authors that the 1977/78 influenza outbreak was caused by viruses incident from space.

Chapter six of the work argues the case for comets being the vehicles by which life was brought to the Earth. The most likely places where the selective pressure exists whereby bacteria can acquire such extreme survival properties is on cometary bodies which undergo the extremities of heat and cold on their highly elliptical and elongated orbits around the sun.

"Viruses from Space" is a truly fascinating book whose interdisciplinary nature should spur the astronomer, the physician, the biologist and the chemist to think outside of their conventional boxes and elevate their respective disciplines to a genuine cosmological scale.

XXXVII

Our Place in the Cosmos:

by Fred Hoyle & Chandra Wickramasinghe

The essential theme of "Our Place in the Cosmos (1993)," by Fred Hoyle and Prof. N. Chandra Wickramasinghe, is the next phase of the ongoing "Copernican Revolution." This revolution, initiated by Nicolas Copernicus, replaced the Earth with the sun as the centre of the Universe. Since the 16th century, heliocentricity has developed in such a way that our sun is now recognised as being just one star among billions in the galaxy and that our galaxy is merely one of countless billions in a vast and expanding universe. Hoyle and Wickramasinghe usher in the next phase of this revolution by taking life out of its terrestrial confines and placing it within a much greater cosmological context. In this respect, they aver that the Darwinian model of evolution, itself pre-Copernican in its postulations, should be ditched and a new model embracing evolution on a cosmological scale be adopted.

If mainstream science and the public at large find the concepts in this book hard to grasp, it is, according to the authors, mainly due to the educational system which discourages inventiveness and originality of thinking, and passes on "....illusions from one generation to the next...." (p. 8).

"Our Place in the Cosmos," is itself an "evolution" from Hoyle's and Wickramasinghe's earlier works on the subject of astrobiology. In "Diseases from Space" (1979), they postulated the theory of bacteria and viruses having their origin in outer space. In "Evolution from Space" (1984), the two scientists averred that household flies and various other insects also were incident from space. "Our Place in the Cosmos," convincingly argues that a great deal of evolutionary activity occurs in space, with the result that most of the trunk of the Tree of Life is to be found outside of the Earth.

Like all of Hoyle's and Wickramasinghe's works, "Our Place in the Cosmos" should be read with an open and unbiased mind. The reader who approaches this book without any educational preconditions or preconceived mental hindrances, will be well rewarded with some fascinating concepts that will enable him to view reality in a very different and much broader light.

XXXVIII

Lectures on Cosmology and Action at a Distance Electrodynamics:

by Fred Hoyle & Jayant Narlikar

"Lectures on Cosmology and Action at a Distance Electrodynamics" by Fred Hoyle and Prof. Jayant V. Narlikar is a highly technical book and most definitely not intended for the uninitiated masses. The basis of the work is to relate the absorber theory developed by Wheeler and Feynam to a cosmological level. The crux of Hoyle's and Narlikar's approach is that it is the Steady State theory rather than the Big Bang theory that satisfies the cosmological boundary conditions. Before elaborating on their theory, Hoyle and Narlikar explain the historical foundations of theoretical physics. They begin with Newton, then go on to Gauss's theories and explain Maxwell's and Faraday's successful unification of electrodynamic forces.

The work is divided into three principle sections: Classical Electrodynamics; Quantum Electrodynamics Non-Relativistic Processes; Relativistic Quantum Electrodynamics. Each subdivision of the section, entitled "Lecture" ends with a series of exercises designed to test students' understanding of the concepts dealt with.

While the book is not intended for a wide readership, it is an excellent source of information for students of physics at university level. It may also provide the stimulus for postgraduate researchers to enquire further into this area of science.

XXXIX

Archaeopteryx: The Primordial Bird:

by Fred Hoyle & Chandra Wickramasinghe

After reading "Archaeopteryx: The Primordial Bird" one can only feel absolutely convinced that the book's subtitle "A case of fossil forgery" is perfectly justified. Fred Hoyle and Professor N. Chandra Wickramasinghe have made a thorough investigation of the fossil housed in the British Museum and have clearly demonstrated that Archaeopteryx cannot possibly have been the forerunner of modern birds. It certainly seems to be a case of what we may term "Piltdown Bird"!

In the first chapter of their book, the two authors examine the origin of birds within an evolutionary context. Here they draw upon their previously expounded theory which essentially places evolution within a cosmic rather than a merely terrestrial dimension. It is within this dimension that the origin of birds are placed, namely by what the authors term "genetic storms" incident upon the Earth from outer space. According to their panspermia theory, it is microbial invasions from space which provide the driving engine of evolution. Genetic storms from space will wipe out much of the existing biological stock. However, by viral material incident from space grafting onto surviving stock, new species will suddenly appear in the fossil record. It is by a grafting process of viral material onto reptilian stock during a genetic storm which occurred at the Cretaceous-Tertiary boundary around sixty five million years ago that gave rise to birds. Archaeopteryx is supposed to have been found in Jurassic strata which dates back 160 million years. This would apparently negate the theory that birds had their origin at the Crataceous-Tertiary boundary. Yet, the authors clearly show that "Archaeopteryx" is nothing more than the dinosaur Compsognathus with modern feathers fraudulently imprinted onto it. The general framework of Hoyle's and Wickramasinghe's investigation into Archaeopteryx is their rejection of the neo-Darwinian account of evolutionary processes.

The bulk of the book is mainly devoted to a detailed technical examination of the fossil, the feathers and the rock in which Archaeopteryx was discovered. It is chiefly by a comparison of slab and counter slab that the authors demonstrate the incongruities which make the Archaeopteryx fossil a highly suspicious artifact. The authors also comment on the skeleton of Archaeopteryx and state that the structure of its anatomy could not possibly have permitted for flight as an option of locomotion for the creature.

Apart from their painstaking scientific investigation of the forgery, Hoyle and Wickramasinghe look closely at the historical background of the "discovery" of "Archaeopteryx" and at the dramatis personae in the play. They note that this fossil came hot on the heels of Darwin 's "Origin of Species" when just such a fossil discovery was predicted. The authors also examine the character and motives of Richard Owen, the Superintendent of the British Museum 's Natural History Section, who bought the fossil on behalf of the Museum. Owen was a vociferous opponent of Charles Darwin's and Thomas Henry Huxley's evolutionary theory and it would seem that Owen acquired the dubious fossil in order to discredit Darwin and Huxley; yet, as the authors clearly point out, this was a ruse that neither Darwin nor Huxley fell for.

This book is a great read for both professional paleontologist and interested lay reader alike. Though many paleontologists still cling to the authenticity of Archaeopteryx, they still have not successfully countered the strong evidence presented by Hoyle and Wickramasinghe that so obviously shows Archaeopteryx to be a fraud.

XL

The Theory of Cosmic Grains:

by Fred Hoyle & N.C. Wickramasinghe

"The Theory of Cosmic Grains" is a highly technical book which is written mainly for the specialist in astronomical (and more specifically, astrobiological) studies and thus may prove to be a somewhat daunting read for the average layman. Nevertheless, the non-specialist who perseveres with the perusal of this work, will obtain a reasonably good grasp of the issue of interstellar grains and a solid grounding in the controversy surrounding their composition.

In the introductory section of the book, the authors, Fred Hoyle and Prof. N. Chandra Wickramasinghe, guide the reader through the history of the attempts which various astronomers had made, since the time of Sir William Herschel, to come to an understanding of the exact nature of this obscuring matter found between the stars.

Hoyle and Wickramasinghe have their main starting point in the decade of the 1930's when the first serious attempts were made to devise theories to explain the nature and composition of interstellar dust. The first six chapters of the book are devoted to demonstrating the inadequacy of the conventional models of interstellar dust - namely the iron grain theory, the ice grain theory, graphite grains and refractory grain mixtures. They show that it is only when astronomers start to consider models involving organic polymers and, more controversially, biological grains, that the spectroscopic evidence can be interpreted in any convincing way. It is from this point that Hoyle and Wickramasinghe expound upon their theory of bacteriological interstellar grains seeding the Universe via comets and cometary related material. In a kind of an aside from the core consideration of this work, they offer an alternative to the standard explanation of the cosmic microwave background radiation (generally interpreted as a remnant of the explosion which Big Bang cosmology holds as being the genesis event in the origin of the Universe) by suggesting that it instead emanates from "iron whiskers" hurled into intergalactic space by supernova explosions.

The issue of interstellar grain composition still remains unresolved twenty four years (at the time of writing) after the publication of this book. Perhaps this is because of ".....the reluctance of cosmologists to think outside the patterns to which they have become accustomed..." (p.290 par.3) and an unwillingness to give reasonable consideration to completely different theoretical models. This thoroughly researched and well referenced book will surely serve as a good starting point for any young aspiring scientist who may wish to steer his scientific endeavours in the direction of astrobiological study and research.

XLI

Life on Mars? A case for Cosmic Heritage?

by Fred Hoyle & Chandra Wickramasinghe

"Life on Mars? The case for a cosmic heritage" is a well researched book authored by the late Fred Hoyle and Professor N. Chandra Wickramasinghe. In this book, the authors essentially develop the theme laid down in their two previous books "Diseases from Space" and "Lifecloud" that life had an extraterrestrial rather than a merely localised terrestrial origin.

Hoyle and Wickramasinghe begin by examining the conditions for life in our solar system. While complex forms of life such as plant and animal species are ruled out, the authors do not dismiss the possibility of simpler microbial life forms surviving in places such as the higher parts of the Venusian atmosphere, the Martian soil and on some of the satellites of Jupiter and Saturn. In the same chapter, consideration is given to the number of Earth - like worlds that may exist on extra-solar planets and how many of these may have developed advanced life and advanced technological civilisations.

When arguing the case for Panspermia(or "Cosmicrobia" as the authors prefer to term the concept) Hoyle and Wickramasinghe point out the fallacies in the arguments against this theory. That microorganisms display an immense capacity to survive ultraviolet light is a fact used by the authors to give substance to their contention that microorganisms can survive the ravages of interstellar space and move from one star system to another. Graphs which show a parallel between the known spectral emission and absorption curves of bacteria and those of interstellar gas clouds are used to strengthen the theory of Panspermia(Cosmicrobia). Comets are considered by the authors as being the vehicles by which life is brought to planets. As comets, in their highly elliptical orbits, approach the sun, they evaporate some of their material - the familiar "tail" of the comet. Much of this material, argue the authors, is biological. As the Earth passes through the debris left by evaporated cometary material, it picks up some of it this debris in the form of viral and bacterial matter.

One of the most interesting themes of this work is the authors' challenge to the classical Darwinian theory of the origin of life. They mathematically prove that life could not have begun on Earth as the resources of a single planet are insufficient to allow for all the possible combinations of the base pairs of DNA needed in order to produce the great variety of life forms. It is essential that life be a cosmic rather than a mere Earth bound phenomenon. It is also of interest to note how Hoyle and Wickramasinghe tie in Panspermia with the Steady State Theory. Just as the Universe, according to this theory, has always existed, so too has life. In arguing the case for Steady State/ Panspermiatheory, the authors state - "which came first, the blueprint for the enzyme or the enzyme itself".

The final part of this book examines the case for various diseases such as influenza, the common cold, mumps and whooping cough being extraterrestrial in origin and brought to the Earth by comets. By using climatological and meteorological data, the two authors present a convincing case for the extraterrestrial origin of influenza outbreaks. They also link this theory of the origin of diseases to their main Panspermia theory by contending that it is from viral and bacterial matter shed by comets that the Earth receives fresh inputs of DNA in order to drive the engine of evolution.

As in all their other works, Fred Hoyle and Professor Wickramasinghe never cease to be controversial. Yet, it is only by controversy that science and technology - and indeed, society itself - can progress. In the epilogue of "Life on Mars", the authors show a compelling connection between major civilizational events and cometary impacts on the Earth. So in terms of the health of mankind and even, dare it be said, the very survival of the human species, we may well be being subliminally advised by the authors of this book to start looking upwards far more often.

XLII

Mathematics of Evolution:

by Fred Hoyle

Although Fred Hoyle's book "Mathematics of Evolution" is not for the layman in that it treats of evolution by the use of highly complex mathematical formulae, the average reader can, nevertheless, through a patient perusal of the work, glean quite a lot of information from it.

One could say that the essence of the book lies in its challenge to what has become known as neo-Darwinism. In the preface to his book, Hoyle makes clear that his opposition to the standard Darwinian model is based upon different premises to the more commonly touted religious objections to the theory. By his statement, "to deny the paleontological evidence of evolution, and in particular, man's place in it, is on a par with denying that water flows downhill" (p.xv), Fred Hoyle does not reject evolution, but rather offers an alternative explanation for its mechanistic functioning. Although Hoyle's career was in the astronomical and cosmological sciences, his interests in biology date back to his student days in the 1930's, when, during his frequent discussions with his contemporary, George Carson, on the subject of Darwinian evolution, Carson, a biology PhD candidate, conferred to Hoyle that " .....something" was "....amiss with the Darwinian theory."

Apart from the deficiency of transitional fossils in the geological record, Hoyle shows, by rigorous mathematical proofs, how the Darwinian model as an explanation for the evolutionary process lacks viability. In "Mathematics of Evolution", Hoyle, as in his other publications of the same genre, accounts for the diversity of biological forms by a means which he, and his colleague, Prof. Chandra Wickramasinghe, term "genetic storms." Placing the issue of evolution within the academic discipline of Astrobiology, a marriage of astronomy and biology, and thus onto a wider cosmological context, biological diversity can be explained by the acquisition of incoming genes by terrestrial species.

Through the process of unifying biology with astronomy, and by further placing the astrobiological theory within a mathematical framework, Hoyle does much in the way of logically filling in the gaps left open by standard Darwinian theory.

XLIII

Astronomical Origins of Life: Steps Towards Panspermia:

by F. Hoyle & N. C. Wickramasinghe

"Astronomical Origins of Life: Steps Towards Panspermia" by Fred Hoyle and Professor N. Chandra Wickramasinghe is composed of a collection of the writings of the two scientists over two decades which writings argue for the origin of life as being a cosmic phenomenon and, as a corollary, evolutionary theory being transferred to an extraterrestrial dimension.

In the preface to their book, Hoyle and Wickramasinghe explain the process by which they came to the conclusion that life begins in outer space. While microevolution is indeed a terrestrial event, the authors contend that the genetic basis of life does not occur on the Earth but instead is a process which goes on throughout the entire Universe. In the introductory chapter entitled "Panspermia", the authors examine the history of the theory and the evidence supporting it in the composition of interstellar dust, cometary material, meteorites and in terrestrial geology. The bulk of the book is divided into six parts, each dealing with an aspect of panspermia theory.

The first section "General Considerations", looks at the chemical basis of life and the conditions in the early solar system, particularly in comets, which could have been congenial to the development of basic genetic material. One chapter is devoted to an interesting experiment which shows how micro-organisms can survive extremes of temperature and could thus conceivably enter the Earth from outer space without any danger to their survival being posed by atmospheric entry conditions. In the chapter which examines biological evolution the two authors take their characteristic swipe at Charles Darwin whom they show as being influenced by the erroneous Lamarckian theory of evolution by natural selection. Hoyle and Wickramasinghe contend that Alfred Russel Wallace conveyed evolutionary theory in greater clarity as he eschewed natural selection and instead argued for the sudden appearance and disappearance of species which Hoyle and Wickramasinghe explain by the input of genetic material from outer space.

In the second section of the book, the authors examine the chemical composition of interstellar dust and comets. They argue that spectroscopic analyses favours the infrared emission as being indicative of polymers and polyformaldehyde rather than of silicates.

Sections four and five of the book are taken up with demonstrating the compatibility of spectral analyses of interstellar grains with the spectral analyses of bacteria. The final section, which deals with comets and life, Hoyle and Wickramasinghe argue the case for comets being the vehicles by which genetic material is distributed around the solar system.

Although this work is extremely technical and aimed mainly at the specialist, the interested layman can still glean enough from between its covers to achieve a sufficient grasp of the basic principles of panspermia theory.

XLIV

A Different Approach to Cosmology: from a Static Universe through the Big Bang towards Reality.

By Fred Hoyle, Geoffrey Burbidge and Jayant V. Narlikar

The tone of "A Different Approach to Cosmology," by Fred Hoyle, Geoffrey Burbidge and Jayant V. Narlikar is set in the book's Introduction whereby the authors lay down their challenge to conventionally accepted ideas concerning the Universe. Citing Agnes Clerke's book "The System of the Stars" (1905) in which the Milky Way galaxy was considered as constituting the entirety of the Universe, and then citing Einstein's fixed notion of a static Universe, the three authors argue their core point that the same type of boxed thinking is prevalent in the scientific community today especially regarding the accepted "fact" of Big Bang cosmology as a means of explaining the Universe.

The format of the book follows a chronological sequence of the development of cosmology from the beginning to the end of the 20th century. The previous century witnessed the development of big science funded by organisations such as NASA in the US and the Science Research Council in the UK. Hoyle, Burbidge and Narlikar claim that scientists utilising the facilities provided by the funding from such like organisations must not only make "extravagant claims" (p. viii in the Preface) regarding what they expect to find, but, that after having conducted their research activities, they have indeed actually found what they expected to find, with the woeful result that "....there is no room for the discovery of phenomena which has not already been expected" (p. viii in the Preface).

The second chapter entitled "Early Relatavistic Cosmology" demonstrates that cosmological thinking during the opening years of the 20th century centredaround a Universe that was static, homogeneous and isotropic. Improvements in observational techniques served to demonstrate the complexity in the structure of the Universe and ".... that the expectations of the 1930's were based upon cosmological models that were too simplistic" (p. 15). The velocity-distance relationship in galactic recession as played out in the dispute between Edwin Hubble and A. Van Maanen are detailed in chapter three of the book. Chapter four deals with the Hubble Constant in relation to the red shift while chapter five examines the advances in radio astronomy since the end of the Second World War. What is notable here is the division of this new science into two groups - one in Cambridge and the other in Manchester, headed by Sir Martin Ryle and Sir Bernard Lovell respectively. Hoyle, Burbidge and Narlikarcriticise the secrecy surrounding the Cambridge group and comment that "open minds and freedom of ideas" were not virtues encouraged within its ranks.

The steady state cosmological model is given great consideration throughout the book. Chapter seven details the rivalry between Hoyle and Ryle regarding the interpretation of the counts of radio sources in the Universe while chapter eight offers the condensation of carbon vapour into long thread like particles as an alternative explanation to the cosmic microwave background radiation. Chapters nine and ten deal mainly with stellar nucleosynthesis as an explanation for the abundance of heavy elements within a steady state Universe.

The rest of the book is mainly concerned with interpreting cosmological phenomena within the context of a steady state model rather than the generally accepted big bang one. This makes the book a refreshing alternative to the conventionally accepted interpretations of the nature of the Universe thus giving the modern day student of astrophysics and cosmology an insight into alternative explanations of cosmological origins, explanations which are both credible and well considered by the three authors.

XLV

Cosmic Life Force: The Power of Life across the Universe.

By Fred Hoyle & Chandra Wickramasinghe

"Cosmic Life Force: The Power of Life across the Universe" by Fred Hoyle and Chandra Wickramasinghe (1990) is a compendium of the many works relating to the pioneering research undertaken by these two authors in the field of Astrobiology. The book's core thesis is that life and its evolution is a cosmically driven force rather than a phenomenon confined to the terrestrial environment.

This fascinating work by Hoyle and Wickramasinghe opens with an overview of the history of life on planet Earth (The Terrestrial Abode – Chapter 1) from its remote beginnings some 3.8 billion years ago, all the way up to the astonishing achievements of modern man. The main thrust of the Hoyle/Wickramasinghe theory of life's evolution and development having to have required the resources of the entire Universe is laid out in their statement – "The fact that the oldest sedimentary rocks on the Earth, which were laid down some 3500 to 3800 million years ago, show the presence of microbial fossils is, in our view, a clear indication that life was added from outside. There was little or no time available for any 'primordial soup' to have brewed on the Earth prior to the time when these sediments were laid down" (p.6) The authors argue, both in this chapter and throughout the book, that comets were the delivery mechanisms whereby life was brought to the Earth and that it was this life which produced the vast stores of energy, mainly in the form of photosynthetic biological matter and fossilised hydrocarbons, that made for the vast industrial and technological leaps and bounds of mankind down through the ages.

Chapter 2 (The Legacy of Comets) continues with the subject of comets and examines man's view of them since early times. What is of particular note in this chapter is that ancient notions of comets being the harbingers of doom may not have been too wide of the mark: Hoyle and Wickramasinghe point out that scientific analyses of comets points to their containing organic compounds and even to their being places where biological activity occurs. A spectrographic analysis which they show for Halley's Comet (Fig.2.3 p.25) indicates a correlation with that for laboratory dried bacteria. This would back up to a great extent the authors' hypothesis that various epidemic diseases originate from bacteria incident from space falling through the Earth's atmosphere. In the following two chapters "The Conquest of the Solar System" and "The Conquest of our Galaxy" - 3 & 4 respectively – Hoyle and Wickramasinghe extend the astrobiological theory of comets to the wider solar system and beyond into the galaxy.

The authors digress somewhat in Chapter 5 (Interstellar Communications) into the more speculative realms of possible communication with intelligent life in our galaxy. They cogently argue that if the seeds of life are dispersed on a cosmic scale, then there is no reason why, given the appropriate conditions, that intelligent life should not have the ability to establish itself on other planets. In this part of their work, the authors consider the possible means by which contact could be made with intelligent extraterrestrial life forms.

In Chapter 6 (The Viral Vector), Hoyle and Wickramasinghe consider the question of evolution as a phenomenon driven by the acquisition by species of fresh genetic material acquired from space incident bacteria falling upon the Earth. They highlight the deficiencies inherent in the Darwinian model which postulates evolution in a purely terrestrial context, and argue that the resources of the cosmos must come into play if species are to evolve to higher levels.

Further evidence to support the contention that new genetic input originates from outer space is given in Chapter 7 (Life Force and Disease) where Hoyle and Wickramasinghe argue the case for space incident viruses and bacteria being the cause of such sicknesses as the common cold and influenza. By examining the incidences of these and other so-called contagious diseases and the patterns of their spread, the authors convincingly make the case for casting serious doubt on the person to person (horizontal) mechanism for the propagation of these epidemics.

Instead, they offer a new model which relies upon vertical movements of the viral and bacterial causative agents whose spread is based upon meteorological and topographical factors.

Most noteworthy in Chapter 8 (The Fabric of the World) is the authors' refutation of Big Bang cosmology in favour of a Steady State model for the Universe. What is of great interest in this section of the book is their interpretation of the microwave background radiation whereby they explain the phenomenon in terms of metallic needles or "whiskers" which are produced in supernovae explosions and flung into inter-galactic space.

In the penultimate chapter (The Control of Galaxies) Hoyle and Wickramasinghe controversially argue the case for the processes of galaxy formation and structure being biologically controlled via bacteria. As, according to their theory, space dust is composed mainly of desiccated bacteria, biological processes will be the main driving force in galaxy formation.

In the final chapter (The Concept of a Creator), the authors discuss the notion of a super-intelligence controlling the Universe. While they acknowledge that the mainstream of science is uncomfortable with this consideration, they argue on the basis of mathematical probability, the high improbability of life being a chance event in its evolutionary context.

Twenty five years after its publication (at the time of writing this review), Cosmic Life Force still remains an amazing read as its concepts have still to find acceptance within mainstream science, yet with mainstream scientific research lending ever increasing degrees of confirmation to its propositions.

XLVI

A Contradiction in the Argument of Malthus:

By F. Hoyle

"A Contradiction in the Argument of Malthus" was the title of a lecture delivered by Sir Fred Hoyle at the University of Hull on 17th May 1963 as the St. John's College Cambridge Lecture speaker for that year.

Most people who are familiar with the arguments laid down by Thomas Malthus regarding the maximum numbers of people that the Earth can sustain take it as axiomatic that Malthus' analysis is beyond dispute. However, on the basis of two propositions, Hoyle convincingly demolishes the Malthusian argument relating food production over levels of human population.

The first of these is that the maintenance of a sophisticated technological society cannot be effected by starving people, while the second is that such a society is able to support its population *".....well above starvation level"* (p.10) whereas societies which are technologically underdeveloped have difficulty sustaining their populations at the level of starvation. Once these two propositions are accepted as being self-evident, the Malthusian argument breaks down. Malthus, failing to take into account scientific and technological advances of the kind mentioned by Hoyle (such as synthetic food, the cultivation of regions hitherto inaccessible to agriculture, the processing and preservation of food), based his theory upon a level of agricultural production at more or less that of subsistence. The irony here is that while Malthusian theory envisages a population level outstripping that of agricultural production, Hoyle's two propositions require a decrease in population in order to attain the levels of a Malthusian state of affairs.

While Hoyle would not contend with Malthus that a population overload would be the trigger for societal collapse, Hoyle differs from Malthus in terms of the actual mechanism for collapse; such a collapse would not ensue from the Malthusian starvation scenario, but from a level of population that permitted no more standing room than one square yard per person. This collapse would increase the death rate due to the fact that the organisational structures designed to feed such a high level of population, would no longer be operational. However, after a massive decrease in the population, the trend towards spiraling population levels would resume: this would eventually cause another collapse followed by yet another population regeneration – and so the cycle of overpopulation followed by collapse followed by population increase would continue.

It is in the consideration of these cycles of overpopulation followed by societal collapse that Hoyle introduces an interesting element into the equation – evolution. At the collapse stage of each cycle, a process of natural selection coming into play would favour those of a higher than average IQ and those most suited to operating within structures which are more socially orientated. This form of "mini-evolution" would, according to Hoyle, after a number of cycles, result in a creature that, while still essentially human, have deviated sufficiently from the current genus to warrant being labeled as a new species.

It is a fair conclusion that, taking into consideration the aforementioned propositions laid down by Hoyle, and his explanation of the biological selection processes inherent in the population cycles he proposes as a result of overpopulation, the theory as espoused by Malthus in his publication, *An Essay on the Principle of Populations as it Affects the Future Improvement of Society* (1798) is now redundant and that future planning involving the close connection between population levels and societal organisational development will have to be based on these longer term considerations rather than merely upon the short-term and immediate requirements of communities.

XLVII

Why Neo- Darwinism Does Not Work:

By Fred Hoyle and Chandra Wickramasinghe

In their essay entitled "Why Neo-Darwinism Does Not Work," Fred Hoyle and Chandra Wickramasinghe, have convincingly shown by mathematical proofs that the Darwinian model of evolution is seriously flawed and in need of revision.

The authors attack what is known as the Hardy-Weinberg theorem and argue that it cannot be used to account for evolutionary change. They find it astonishing that G.H. Hardy allowed neo-Darwinians "…. to misinterpret the probability calculated in his theorem as if it were a fact" (p.12). That Hardy overlooked this obvious distinction is something that can be explained from a sociological rather than mathematical/ scientific perspective – the sociological issue being the ingrained belief in the Darwinian model of evolution. Hoyle and Wickramasinghe also contend that acceptance of Darwin's theory has been the cause of much human suffering when misapplied in the political sphere.

Hoyle and Wickramasinghe subscribe to the theory that successful adaptations of certain creatures to their respective environments is the result of the "…breadth of the initial gene pool…".(p.22) rather than being the outcome of genetic mutation. Evolution by natural selection processes in the way of random shuffling of amino acids is pitted against massive odds – in the region of 1040 000. Within the framework of the argument that evolution occurs because "Biological systems….. are not closed…." (p.25) the authors, with reference to their previously published works on this theory (e.g. *Evolution from Space,* Dent, 1981), here enunciate their theory that genetic input in the dynamic of evolution is a cosmologically wide rather than merely a terrestrial phenomenon.

Hoyle and Wickramasinghe conclude their work by the amazing claim that the mathematical disproof of the Darwinian model could have been demonstrated from as early as 1859, and that it has constantly been ignored by generations of mathematicians is something they put down to "….intellectual perversity…." (p.33) resulting in "…..mass delusion….." (p.33) an outcome they fear will go beyond the bounds of the biological sciences and engender a more widespread deleterious effect on "…..every aspect of modern society" (p. 33).

Part III

Works with a Forward by Fred Hoyle.

Contents

I) Fundamental Studies and the Future of Science: *Forward by Fred Hoyle. Edited by Prof. N. C. Wickramasinghe* 123

II) Space and Eternal Life: A Dialogue between Chandra Wickramasinghe and Daisaku Ikeda. *Forward by Sir Fred Hoyle* 125

III) An Introduction to Cosmology. *By Professor Jayant Vishnu Narlikar: with a Forward by Sir Fred Hoyle* 127

I

Fundamental Studies and the Future of Science:

Forward by Fred Hoyle.

Edited by Prof. N. C. Wickramasinghe

It may seem somewhat strange to begin a review of "Fundamental Studies and the Future of Science," (edited by Professor N. Chandra Wickramasinghe) with the entry by J.R. Jayewardene, a one time president of Sri Lanka. However, considering that it was President Jayewardene's idea to set up the Institute of Fundamental Studies in 1981, and considering that his speech sums up the tone of the inaugural lectures (upon which this book is based) at the launch of this Institute, the appropriateness of starting with the speech of a politician may not seem so inappropriate after all. President Jayewardene expressed his hope that the Institute would "fulfill its objectives by contributing to the expanding of man's knowledge of himself and the Universe around him."

It is this hope of the President that is reflected in the thirty lectures delivered by whom he refers to as the "....men and women, famous throughout the world for their intellectual attainments and their contributions to fundamental studies in varied fields of human knowledge" (p.271). The very title of President Jayewardene's speech - "Science, Politics and Yogic Traditions" (pp.271 - 274)- itself shows that though human knowledge be diverse, there is nevertheless, an interconnecting thread running through all the disciplines into which that knowledge is generally academically compartmentalised. The great need and importance of the Institute of Fundamental Studies is articulated by President Jayewardene in his acknowledgement of the fact that so many of the problems which afflict the world cannot be solved by the politician alone, but instead require a close co-operative working relationship between those engaged in the scientific and political arenas (P. 271). In his forward to this tome, Fred Hoyle states ".... that our technical attainments have run ahead of our capacity to understand them" (p.vii) with the result that much input will be required from those operating in such fields as sociology and philosophy. In the first of the inaugural lectures entitled "On the causes of Plate Tectonics" (pp.1 -23), Fred clearly demonstrates the close relationship between biological and geological activities. Fred Hoyle and Professor N. C. Wickramasinghe in their paper "Interstellar Grains: Dogmas, Trends and Refutations (pp.320 - 341) and in the paper "The Survival of E.Coli Under Extremely High Pressures," by Al Mufti, Hoyle, and Wickramasinghe, (pp. 342 - 352) show the interconnectedness of life and the much wider cosmos. Hoyle and Wickramasinghe bring the epidemiological branch of medicine into a greater cosmic dimension by convincingly arguing in their paper "The Anatomy of a Conference Epidemic" (pp. 386 - 390) that cold and influenza viruses are incident from space.

Contributions from Sir Arthur C. Clarke, "War and Peace in the Space Age" (pp.275 - 284), R.S. Ramakrishna, "Chemical Sciences and Resources Development" (pp. 161 - 172) and "Medicinal Plant Research: Retrospect and Prospect," by L.B. De Silva (pp. 192 - 210) are examples of the diversity and unity of human knowledge so clearly shown by this inaugural seminar.

It is to be sincerely hoped that after 32 years (at the time of writing in 2013) of operation, the Institute of Fundamental Studies, based in a country where, as President Jayewardene has pointed out, "four of the great religions have made ....their home," has been at the forefront of advancing what this writer would term as the greatest, yet most overlooked facet of human knowledge, which is that human knowledge is interconnected into a great cosmic oneness.

II

Space and Eternal Life: A Dialogue between Chandra Wickramasinghe and Daisaku Ikeda.

Forward by Sir Fred Hoyle

Before one has even read the very first sentence of this book, a sense of awe will surely have already been engendered by the very title of the book itself. And as the reader makes his way through the first few pages of this work, soon to overcome him will be an abundant awareness that consideration of such a breathtaking topic as space and eternal life could not have been undertaken by more able scholars and incisively sharp intellects as are possessed by Chandra Wickrmasinghe and Daisaku Ikeda.

Chandra Wickramasinghe brings his skills as both poet and astronomer to introduce the reader to haiku poetry which he describes as ".....having a quality that might be described as 'cosmic'" (page 4). Fred Hoyle, who composed an introduction to "Space and Eternal Life," often contended that the divisions imposed by academia on the sciences were purely artificial but for which Nature has no respect. The highly intellectual dialogue between Wickramasinghe and Ikeda, upon which this book is based, extends Hoyle's analysis into the arts, humanities and philosophical/religious domains. These interconnections are manifested where Wickramasinghe argues that the poet and the scientist, using different language, "...discern the truths hidden in the facts" (page 7). The overlap of cosmology and religion is dealt with (page 32) where Ikeda equates the Buddhist view of the nature of the Universe with modern day observations and empirical scientific models of its structure. The interconnectedness of the academic disciplines is elevated to a higher level where Wickramasinghe and Ikeda contrast the reductionism of the Cartesian approach to reality with that of the more holistic dependent origination view inherent in the Buddhist mindset (pages 64 - 70).

It is from the perspective of the Eastern world view that the two scholars, using a variety of both modern and historical sources, extend their dialogue to cover issues as diverse as medicine, ecology, pacifism, nuclear proliferation, education and the sanctity of the family as the basic unit of society. As Buddhist teaching fuses the inner cosmos of the human mind with the physical structures of the external Universe, the science of astronomy has a major role to play in fostering a truly human awareness among peoples for the purpose of ensuring a genuine global peace (pages 215 - 222).

With conflicts raging throughout the world and peace seemingly as elusive as ever, "Space and Eternal Life" is an apropos read for all who are genuinely desirous of world peace and who care for the welfare of their fellow human beings. Whatever field in which one may be engaged - whether it be in the arts, sciences, medicine or philosophy - this significant contribution by Wickramasinghe and Ikeda can quite convincingly be seen as the tool they have provided by which the practitioner may elevate his academic endeavours to a plane whereby he will be better enabled to apply the works of his vocation to the greater cause of humanity's betterment.

III

An Introduction to Cosmology.

By Professor Jayant Vishnu Narlikar: with a Forward by Sir Fred Hoyle

In his forward to the new third edition of "An Introduction to Cosmology" by Professor Jayant Vishnu Narlikar, Fred Hoyle avers that this work of Narlikar's is "important" both for the student and the "practiced expert." A "masterpiece of clarity" this well structured book is divided into twelve chapters each containing its own sub-sections and a series of exercises for the reader to perform. Perhaps the most salient, and indeed, refreshing aspect of this work is that it does not blindly accept big bang cosmology as a "given" but renders consideration to the steady state model as a way of accounting for cosmological phenomena. The association between Hoyle and Narlikar is shown in the subsection "The Hoyle-Narlikar cosmologies" of Chapter 8 entitled "Alternative cosmologies." The Steady State Theory and the quasi Steady State Theory are given due consideration in subsections 9.2 and 9.10 respectively of Chapter 9. In subsection 9.13.2 (pps. 354 – 358), Narlikar explains the Hoyle-Wickramasinghe alternative to the conventional account of the micro-wave background radiation, the conventional model explaining this phenomenon as a remnant of the Big Bang, but which is accounted for by Hoyle and Wickramasinghe as emanating from metalicvapours condensing into whiskers. This book is not intended for the lay reader, but rather for advanced students and upwards and presumes a knowledge of various mathematical disciplines on the part of the reader.

PART IV

Fiction

Contents

I) Nightmare for Number 10: *Fred Hoyle (*under pseudonym *James Warboys)* 133
II) The Black Cloud: *Fred Hoyle* 134
III) Ossian's Ride: *Fred Hoyle* 136
IV) 'A' for Andromeda: *Fred Hoyle& John Elliot* 138
V) Fifth Planet: *Fred Hoyle& Geoffrey Hoyle* 140
VI) October the First is Too Late: *Fred Hoyle* 142
VII) Andromeda Breakthrough: *Fred Hoyle& John Elliot* 144
VIII) Element 79: *Fred Hoyle* 146
IX) Rockets in Ursa Major: *Fred Hoyle & Geoffrey Hoyle* 148
X) Seven Steps to the Sun: *Fred Hoyle & Geoffrey Hoyle* 150
XI) The Molecule Men: *Fred Hoyle & Geoffrey Hoyle* 152
XII) The Inferno: *Fred Hoyle & Geoffrey Hoyle* 155
XIII) Into Deepest Space: *Fred Hoyle & Geoffrey Hoyle* 157
XIV) The Incandescent Ones: *Fred Hoyle & Geoffrey Hoyle* 159
XV) The Westminster Disaster: *Fred Hoyle &Geoffrey Hoyle* 161
XVI) The Energy Pirate: *Fred Hoyle & Geoffrey Hoyle* 163
XVII) The Frozen Planet of Azuron: *Fred & Geoffrey Hoyle* 164
XVIII) The Giants of Universal Park: *Fred & Geoffrey Hoyle* 166
XIX) The Planet of Death: *Fred & Geoffrey Hoyle* 167
XX) Comet Halley: *Fred Hoyle* 169

I

Nightmare for Number 10:

by Fred Hoyle under pseudonym James Warboys.

What happens when you put all together a knighted JP, his somewhat rebellious son and daughter, a quintessential British county bobby, two quintessential civil servants from government ministries, an Eastern Bloc spy and his rather dull-witted assistant, a truly cerebral professor, a farmer and his wife and their son, an unconventional schoolgirl, and an Inspector from a ministry and his fancy woman? Well, you get a truly hilarious comedy by the name of "Nightmare for Number 10" which would not be out of place at a Christmas festivity – the only difference being that this one would be enjoyed to the fullest by both adults and children alike.

Written under the pseudonym "James Warboys", Fred Hoyle has created a marvelously clever piece of satire whereby these diverse characters descend upon Punch Farm for reasons that are as ridiculously varied as stealing atomic secrets, destroying atomic secrets, poaching fish on the river, trafficking in ration books and claiming on winter sugar feed for non-existent bees. With arson attacks on the Kremlin and the Pentagon being given equal weight to the catching of a predatory fish by the combined efforts of the JP and the farmer, the momentum of the story's hilarity is maintained to the end.

Though a serious scientist of the highest calibre, Hoyle never lost his good old Yorkshire sense of humour, which in real guffaw form, comes out in this cleverly constructed little comedy.

II

The Black Cloud:

by Fred Hoyle

Peter Green's review of "The Black Cloud" in the Daily Telegraph (1957) describes Fred Hoyle's first novel as "... science fiction at its highest level." However, when one reads through this story, the decision as to its classification as fact or fiction becomes a difficult one. Indeed, Green states in his review ".... that the reader feels these events may actually happen."

A close analysis of the book has led me to consider this work as being essentially science fact superimposed upon a background of fiction. The characters and the events are of course purely fictional, but the science that they are involved in comes across as solid and sound.

A group of astronomers at Mount Wilson Observatory in California discover a gaseous cloud in the constellation of Orion. Their calculations show that it is heading towards the solar system. Its speed and position are delineated by diagrams and complex mathematical formulae which are no doubt beyond the average reader. This should not present any justification for criticism of the author as it would appear that Hoyle's intention at this early stage was to set the general tone of the novel which throughout its course presents perfectly cogent arguments for the physical phenomena induced by the Cloud when it eventually enters the solar system.

For those who are familiar with Fred Hoyle's works and career, it is very easy to see the opinions of the author being conveyed through the novel's dramatis personae, most particularly in the central character, Chris Kingsley, professor of astronomy at Cambridge University. When it comes to the time when the political authorities must be informed of the approach of the Cloud and the meteorological consequences of such, Hoyle presents the readers with a dialectic between the archaic and inappropriate responses on the part of the politicians and the practical and sensible measures advocated by the scientific community. The core message in the scenes where Kingsley is in bitter dispute with the Prime Minister and his secretary, is, that the structures and functions of government are lagging far behind the rate of scientific progress.

The terrestrial havoc brought about by the Cloud's proximity to the Earth can be seen as a foretaste of Hoyle's later works on the consequences of climate change. In particular, it foreshadows his 1981 book "Ice - The Ultimate Human Catastrophe" in which Hoyle convincingly argues the case for an impending ice age. The Cloud's blocking out of the sun and radiation from the Cloud, serve to alternately cool and heat the Earth to extreme degrees. In "Ice", the next ice age, though not started by anything quite so dramatic as a Cloud, nevertheless has a cosmic catalyst in the form of a gigantic meteor crashing onto the Earth.

The novel's greatest surprise, that the Cloud actually possesses intelligence, is highly indicative of Hoyle's later theories about life being a cosmic phenomenon rather than as something which evolved solely on planets. Along with his colleague, Chandra Wickramasinghe, Hoyle developed the new academic discipline of astrobiology. Hoyle and Wickramasinghe argued that organic compounds and even bacteria have their origins in interstellar gas clouds. Hoyle postulated the highly controversial theory that many epidemics come from bacteria which enter the Earth's atmosphere from outer space.

Though written in 1957, does the novel have any relevance today or in the future? It surely does, for the detailed description of the consequences of the Earth encountering some form of disruptive astronomical body and the measures outlined for dealing with such a horrendous situation, make this book nothing less than an essential instruction manual which all civil authorities ought to have at hand.

III

Ossian's Ride:

by Fred Hoyle

Fred Hoyle was not only an eminent scientist but also a brilliant science fiction writer. "Ossian's Ride" however is not a typical science fiction book. What gives this novel its added quality is Hoyle's superb ability to weave through a plot composed of a clever synthesis of fiction, science and mystery his knowledge of science and mathematics - but in a way which does not overwhelm the uninitiated and the non-specialist. If "unputdownability", "pickupability" and "pageturnability" are to be the criteria for the judgement of a novel's success, then "Ossian's Ride" passes all three tests with flying colours. The story combines the detective thriller style of an Agatha Christie with the science fiction of an Arthur C. Clarke or an Isaac Asimov. It is this combination of a variety of literary devices which ensures for the reader an exciting and suspense-filled drama from beginning to end. There is simply never a dull moment in the book.

Those who have read Fred's autobiography "Home is Where the Wind Blows" and Simon Mitton's biography of Hoyle "Conflict in the Cosmos", and have thus familiarized themselves with the life of Hoyle, will hardly fail to notice so much of Fred Hoyle in the novel's central character, Thomas Sherwood. Sherwood's great academic abilities and his love of fell walking reflect the author's student days in Cambridge and his life-long passion for fell walking - Hoyle managed to climb all the Munros of Scotland during his life. Since Ireland was so often a holiday destination for Hoyle and his family, it should come as no surprise that most of "Ossian's Ride" takes place in that country and that the scenes where a mysterious canon regales Sherwood and some others with ghost stories are very much to be considered as a tribute to Hoyle's friend Monsignor Paddy Brown who always had a good stock of tales of the supernatural and the unknown with which to tickle the ears of his avid listeners. The incident of the cat, which apparently from no-where, jumps out from among the sparks of the fire in the dimly-lit Irish pub, is as much a scare to the reader as it is to Sherwood and his companions - not to mention the canon who is in the middle of relating one of his ghost stories when the creature makes its abrupt and unannounced entrance! When Thomas Sherwood observes how boxes of fish at the quay in Kilkee are being removed from the fishing boats to the waiting lorries, and how, from these observations, he manages to work out a more efficient mechanism for this procedure, one can descry the young Hoyle truanting from school and gaining knowledge of the principles of engineering and mechanics during his clandestine visits to the mills and canals then so prevalent in the Yorkshire of his day.

Like Hoyle's other science fiction works, "Ossian's Ride" is not totally divorced from science fact. Thomas Sherwood has been briefed by the British Government to get to the bottom of an industrial complex in Ireland which appears to be way in advance of anything for which contemporary science and industry can account. This backdrop to the story is a reminder of Hoyle's early career as a young scientist working on the development of radar at a secret research location during the war. The strange beginning of the novel and its astonishing and unexpected conclusion show us the Hoyle who never desisted from sticking his neck out and offering the unconventional and the unorthodox as alternative explanations for many of the great questions which present not only wonder and awe to scientists but over which all humanity ponders. Perhaps the incident with the cat emerging from the flames of the fire is an analogy of how the things we so often consider as being perpetually confined to the realms of science fiction can so unexpectedly shock us in their sudden transformation to the world of science fact.

IV

'A' for Andromeda:

by Fred Hoyle and John Elliot

"'A' For Andromeda" is a thrilling science fiction book,derived from the BBC television series, co-authored by Fred Hoyle and John Elliot. It consists of 174 pages and is divided into 12 chapters.

Science fiction, mystery and intrigue are combined and woven into a plot which ensures that there is not a page in the book which is free of suspense and excitement. The story opens with a state-of-the-art radio telescope at Bouldershaw Fell picking up a strange signal from the Andromeda Galaxy. Analysis of the signal clearly demonstrates its artificiality. When Dr. John Fleming, the central character in the story, deciphers the signal, it turns out that it has come from an intelligence superior to that of the human mind. The message from Andromeda consists of a set of instructions for creating artificial life. In order to implement these instructions, Fleming demands nothing less than the best computer Britain has to offer. This computer turns out to be located at the rocket research establishment at Thorness in the western isles of Scotland. After initial trial and error, the computer succeeds in creating a beautiful young woman who is aptly named Andromeda. She proves to be of very high intellect, and as such, possesses the ability to absorb information in a fraction of the time it would take a normal human being.

We can discern in this story a common theme which runs through most of Hoyle's novels - a dialectic between science and politics. In his novels, Hoyle indicates his personal frustration with politicians by endowing his principle characters with an impatience bordering upon contempt for government and political processes: Chris Kingsley fulfilled this role in "The Black Cloud", Thomas Sherwood in "Ossian's Ride" and John Fleming fits the bill admirably in " 'A' For Andromeda"; the Minister of Science being referred to as "His Ministership" is an example of how Fleming persistently conveys his contempt for politicians. The political backdrop to the novel is quite clearly the Cold War. The novel's year of publication witnessed the Cuban missile crisis in which a standoff between the Soviet Union and the West threatened to escalate into nuclear conflict. The authors' portrayal of Britain as a nation whose independent options in terms of defence and foreign policy are slipping steadily from its grasp can, with hindsight, be seen as prophetic.

Hoyle and Elliot have in fact laced their novel with many prophesies. It is these prophetic touches which make this novel as exciting and as relevant today as it was in the 1960's and 1970's. Some of what was science fiction then has now materialised into science fact. The computer's electrocution of Christine and its making use of her DNA in the creation of Andromeda is clearly a foreshadowing of cloning. The ability of missiles to find their target is what we would nowadays call "smart weapons". Hoyle in fact proposed these as far back as the end of the Second World War but his concept of "intelligent weapons" at that time was pooh-poohed by the Admiralty. New tissue applied to Andromeda's severely burned hands prefigures modern skin grafting techniques.

What gives this novel an additional layer of fascination are the parts which still remain science fiction. Creating living organisms from non-living components still elude us. A synthesis of computer technology and biology to create conscious artificial intelligence seems as of yet to be some way off into the future. In his 1964 lecture "Of Men and Galaxies" and in his book of the same title, Hoyle considered the possibility of creating an artificial human being. While so far we have not developed techniques by which the aging process can be slowed down, these are nevertheless the subject of serious scientific research. And though Hoyle firmly believed that we are not alone in the Universe, those who are involved in the ongoing SETI programme still await a signal which originates from an intelligent source. It is though, these unfulfilled predictions which make the novel not only a gripping read but a means of showing the careful reader that it is as relevant today as it was at the time when it was written.

V

Fifth Planet:

by Fred Hoyle & Geoffrey Hoyle

In the preface to their novel "Fifth Planet", Fred Hoyle and Mr. Geoffrey Hoyle state that "It is hardly possible to foresee the shape of society a century or more ahead of one's own time, and we have not attempted to do so". The context of the novel is the Cold War and the rivalry between East and West. Yet only 27 years after the novel was written, the Soviet Union collapsed and the Cold War ceased. Yet, so many of the events described in the novel still remain in the far future. They may or may not come true; time alone will tell.

The main action of the story concerns a star named Helios, slightly more massive than the sun, which, with its retinue of planets, is heading towards the vicinity of our solar system. Spectroscopic analysis of one of its planets, Achilles, indicates an Earth like atmosphere. Both East and West send expeditions to Achilles in order to discover as much as possible about the planet. In spite of the rivalry between the Soviets and the West, there turns out to be an astonishing level of co-operation between the two expeditions. When the Western spacecraft loses contact with the Earth, the Soviet spacecraft generously sends the Western crew details of the orbit of Achilles. Although the Soviets are the first to land on Achilles, their craft lands in such a lopsided fashion that it would be impossible for them to leave the planet. The Western crew, who land their craft successfully, offer to take the Russians back home. Together, both Soviets and Westerners explore the planet. Many strange and mysterious things happen during the exploration of the planet, most notably the discovery of a structure which looked liked two bill-boards pulsating with light. One of the main characters in the story, Mike Fawsett, is stricken by a mysterious illness which causes extreme delirium. Eventually, the remaining members of the crew start on their homeward journey towards the Earth.

What gives this novel its distinctive characteristic is the interweaving of science fiction, science fact, Cold War politics, the human psyche, and adulterous relationships. The central character, Hugh Conway, constantly has to deal with his wife Cathy's extramarital affairs with Mike Fawsett. When Fawsett eventually dies of the illness he contracted on Achilles, Conway notices a most peculiar change in Cathy's personality and behaviour. Hugh Conway then starts to suffer from hallucinations which he eventually discovers come from Cathy's manipulation of the memories stored in his brain. He further discovers that Cathy's body has been invaded by the same mysterious force which had been inside Mike Fawsett. It turns out that the structure which the astronauts had discovered on Achilles was a "personality bank". "Cathy" explained to Conway that no-one ever really dies as the phenomenon that is called "life" is an irregularity in a wave surface which appears like a standing wave in the four dimensional structure of the human body. When the body dies the waves dissipate and become lost. The inhabitants of Achilles had found a way to hold the fields after the death of the body. The personality (or wave structure) that had used Fawsett to come to Earth now uses Cathy as a means by which it may return to Achilles.

Perhaps the most profound aspect of this novel is not so much the plot or the science and sex but the most fundamental questions regarding humans both as to how they function as individuals and as societies. If the novel causes us to think deeply about these matters we will surely turn our minds in the direction of who we are, why we are here and what our relationship is with the wider cosmos in which we find ourselves. We will surely wonder at the nature of society which the authors claim is based upon an idea, an idea which does not take too much to shake. We essentially see what we are conditioned to see by our own individual experiences but also as individuals within the collective consciousness of a wider society. So it is that when "Cathy" manipulates the memories of whole societies conditioned by Cold War politics, rockets and atomic weapons are "seen" raining down on cities and wreaking widespread death and destruction. In the same way, for the military personnel standing guard to the rocket at a launching pad, "Cathy" makes it possible for them to see papers with "yum yum it's Halibut's dehydrated kippers" and "Porky's Sausages" as military passes for the launching site! This indicates yet another great profundity in the novel, the good old Yorkshire wit of the Hoyles!

VI

October the First is Too Late:

by Fred Hoyle

For anyone familiar with Fred Hoyle's novels, the first thing that would come over as striking whilst reading "October The First Is Too Late" is that the narrator is a musician rather than a scientist. The story is conveyed in the first person singular by Richard who is a world renowned musician. The other main character in the story is John Sinclair, a physicist. As well as being a scientist, Hoyle was a music lover and had a passion for fell walking. Both Richard and Sinclair are enthusiastic fell walkers. In his novels, Hoyle conveys his personality to his readers through central characters who are top notch scientists. In "October The First Is Too Late", the personality of Hoyle is spread between the two characters Richard (we are not given his surname) and John Sinclair – the musician and the scientist respectively, yet it is the musician who takes centre stage. This is an interesting departure of literary style on the part of Hoyle.

All the chapters in the novel are given musical names such as fugue, adagio and intermezzo. The novel begins with a Preface. Throughout all his adventures Richard spends much of his time trying to convey his feelings, brought on by the most bizarre experiences, through the composition of musical scores.

The theme of the story is concerned with the essence of time and the age old question as to what precisely it is. John Sinclair is called to the Jet Propulsion Laboratories in the United States to help solve the problem of a strange infrared beam with a modulation of one hundred megacycles that appears to be coming from the sun and is interfering with the instrumentations of the JPLs rockets. Some scientists reported that their equipment had shown some seismic disturbances which had gone on for four days but which were undetectable to normal ears. It is then that the novel's most bizarre events take place. Planes fly over the United States yet detect no cities or any other signs of modern civilization. Richard, Sinclair, and their friends fathom out that the inexplicable infrared beam and the intense seismic activity have caused a juxtaposition of historical eras; this has served to create a world in which various regions are in the past and future relative to the novel's present of 1966. Only Britain remains in 1966.

The main thing that we learn from the novel is that time is essentially an illusion. Commonly, we imagine it as running linearly from past to present and on into the future. Yet this is not necessarily so. John Sinclair explains to Richard the nature of time by a pigeon-hole analogy. Different epochs of time are represented by each pigeon hole. Yet one could go from one pigeon-hole to another in non-numerical sequence. Related to time, we could visit different parts of our lives in non-chronological sequence without even knowing it as each part (represented as a pigeon-hole in the analogy) constitutes the present. It is our subjective consciousness that gives the impression of time as an ever-rolling stream.

The novel is a real roller-coaster which has us jumping about from past to future. Britain is still in 1966 but Europe has been thrust back to 1917 where the Great War continues to rage. Greece has reverted to Classical times and Russia and America are six thousand years into the future. Yet, no matter what era the novel takes us to, music is always there. We can quite easily be given the impression that music is truly the universal language not only in terms of geographical and linguistic barriers but over entire swathes of time. And so the novel ends with a Coda.

VII

Andromeda Breakthrough:

by Fred Hoyle & John Elliot

"Andromeda Breakthrough", again derived from the BBC television series, is basically a continuation of Fred Hoyle's and John Elliot's preceding novel, "A for Andromeda". Readers of "A for Andromeda" will be pleased about the sequel as it answers a number of questions the first novel left unanswered. Without a doubt, readers will have wanted to find out exactly what the message was from the Andromeda Galaxy. In the first novel, we are left somewhat up in the air as to who Kaufman is and what the nature of the organisation(Intel) for which he works is. What about the girl Andromeda? Did she survive or not? Fred Hoyle and John Elliot elucidate all this in "Andromeda Breakthrough".

"Andromeda Breakthrough" is essentially a novel which deals with the inherent weaknesses of human beings. It is a novel which draws together the negative forces residing in humanity - power hunger, greed for the filthy lucre, criminality, the shortcomings of the political and scientific establishments - as well as the positive desires which drive Man to better the lot of his species - love, altruism, enlightenment and survival – all to make for an exciting and fast moving epic.

The characters in the first novel are developed more fully in the sequel. Dr. John Fleming is portrayed as a scientist of great intelligence and highly devoted to his work, yet who displays a totally human love and care for the girl constructed artificially according to instructions in the message from the Andromeda Galaxy. There is Professor Madeleine Dawnay, the "de-sexed biochemical genius from Edinburgh", and the almost too-bad-to-be-true Herr Kaufman.

Throughout the novel, the authors keep their readers in suspense over what is perhaps the story's core question – does the Andromeda girl and the unknown message which she carries represent good or evil? In the end, the mystery is revealed and John Fleming is left with a contentious moral choice – to opt to put the human species on an evolutionary path which ultimately leads to its members becoming motionless brains and sightless intelligences, or to maintain the species' essential humanity and prolong its collective suffering to a culminating point which is extinction. Here is no clear cut choice for the student of Moral Philosophy! Perhaps Fleming's decision to go for enlightenment is the result of the maturation of his love for the girl Andromeda who, though constructed according to the design instructions of a vastly superior intelligence, displays all the qualities of a human being. It would appear to be that it is the blending of these two extremes – one representing survival and soullessness, the other, representing humanity and extinction – which creates the via media of human soul survival. It seems to achieve the unachievable - the miraculous merger of sheer science with the "fuzziness" of moral philosophy. Surely it is the product of this apparently "unholy alliance" that the discerning 'exegete" of this novel can interpret as being the greatest, most astonishing, and, above all, true Andromeda Breakthrough. Simply put, it boils down to what the Romans understood thousands of years ago, omniavincitamor – love conquers all. Without the love between John Fleming and the girl Andromeda, this true Breakthrough could never have happened. It is reflective also of Hoyle's disregard for what he saw as the artificial barriers dividing the academic disciplines. This novel shows that it is when we break down barriers that we can really begin the construction process.

Like all of Hoyle's novels, there comes across in "Andromeda Breakthrough," yet another blend – science fact and science fiction. This eerie feeling of reality in the fiction is conveyed by the authors' practical description of the scientific, political and bureaucratic machinery that would have to be mobilised to cope with the kind of emergency depicted in the novel. Hoyle and Elliot have therefore written, within the context of science fiction, a moral and practical guidebook to deal with conceivable science fact.

VIII

Element 79:

by Fred Hoyle

"Element 79" actually consists of 15 short stories. Although their characters and plots are not interconnected, there is, nevertheless, a common theme which runs through these stories which is that mankind is manipulated by superior forces above and beyond the powers of human perception and control. The first of these stories, "Zoomen," is about a number of humans who are kidnapped, apparently at random, and whisked off in a spaceship destined for another planet in another solar system. However, when one of the kidnapped humans, a Hindu named Daghri, is returned to Earth, it is then discovered that the aliens had not acted randomly at all in their selection of humans; Daghri had never harmed or eaten an animal in his life. Only those who had mistreated animals were taken. Was this a way of giving those who ill-use animals a taste of their own medicine?

In the story "Pym makes his point", we see a latter day Faust doing a deal with the Devil. Professor Pym, a retired physicist, had never made any real impact in his field of specialisation. Yet, when the Devil wagers that Pym is incapable of making a wish that would leave a permanent mark on the world, Pym outmaneuvers his satanic visitor and gains the papers he needs to present to the Institute of Physics - papers which would ensure his place among the greats in the world of science.

The story "A Play's the thing" explores the deep recesses of the human mind and shows that writers who are treating on the pathological aspects of humanity do not use structure and logic in their compositions. Rather, the writer is seeking to exercise the basic human need to dominate ".... if not flesh and blood, well at least the figments of his own imagination."

"Cattle Trucks" is a highly amusing story of the Greek god, Dionysius, who jettisons himself to 20th century California and gets himself into all sorts of trouble due to the strangeness of modern technology. He beats up a traffic cop, rapes a couple of air hostesses on a plane, kills the president of the airline company and wrecks an airport.

If anyone is looking for a metaphor of how a nation is spoiled by the pursuit of the illusion of wealth and "development", then "Welcome to slippage city" would fit the bill perfectly. And for those who like the proverbial twist in the tale, "Agent 39" is the story to get into for it comes as a surprise to the reader when it is revealed who the real aliens are and who exactly are steering the UFOs.

"The Martians" is much more in the Hoyle genre of science fiction as this story is given a healthy over-lair of science fact. It is this particular literary device which makes Fred Hoyle's science fiction stories so riveting and unputdownable. One cannot fail to see the prophetic nature of the last of these stories "The operation". It would be difficult for the reader to deny that Hoyle was, once again, ahead of his time in predicting future science fact through what was, at the time he was writing, still, to a great extent in the realms of the imagination. The convergence of man and machine, and the manipulation of humans by what we would now term micro-chip technology, all seem so uncannily like what we now take for granted in the second decade of the new millennium. Hoyle never liked what he called "big science". He saw in it, and in the burgeoning of the "education industry", corporate forms of thinking causing an accompanying loss of individuality and the original thinking which had given rise to the great discoveries in science. "The operation" epitomises Hoyle's concerns along these lines and provides a warning as to where society may be heading.

IX

Rockets in Ursa Major:

by Fred Hoyle & Geoffrey Hoyle.

(Based on a play written for teenage children).

Fred Hoyle and Geoffrey Hoyle have produced a high standard of science fiction in their novel "Rockets in Ursa Major". What makes this work of such high quality is not only its combination of science fiction with science fact but also its tremendous foresightedness.

First published in 1969, "Rockets in Ursa Major" tells the story of a space crew who, under suspended animation in an ice-box, are sent on a course to Ursa Major to explore that part of the galaxy. Contact with the spaceship is lost but to everyone's surprise, it returns thirty years later – but with the crew missing!

Soon, it is discovered that enemy alien spaceships are entering the solar system and plans are set afoot to deal with the threat. A battle ensues but the Earth fleet is beaten. The main character, Dr. Richard Warboys, and a colonel of the Earth fleet, are rescued by the aliens whose visit turns out to have been in friendship. They came for the purpose of warning the Earth that another galactic civilisation known as the Yela are on their way to burn up the Earth. The friendly aliens ally with World Space HQ to beat the Yela in their attempts to sabotage the Earth.

The space battles with the Yela are described in somewhat technical terms involving radar and guided ballistic terminology. This no doubt comes from Fred Hoyle's pioneering work in the development of radar during the years of the Second World War. What is essentially being done in this part of the story is the transference of ballistic science to wars in outer space.

It is interesting to note that short distance travel within the United Kingdom is undertaken by helicopter. The helicopters are computer guided, the driver putting in the punch card appropriate for the particular destination. These helicopter transport scenes may well be considered as a foreseeing of satellite navigation which we are all familiar with in the opening years of the twenty first century. There is surely no-one who could fail to realise that if this form of transportation were common, our current traffic congestion problems would be so much eased. Computerised key systems and automated "waiterless" restaurants all featured in this novel. When one of the characters, Sir John Fielding, goes into a phone booth, the reader may at this point realise that the Hoyles had not anticipated mobile phones!

If one has read other novels by the Hoyles prior to reading "Rockets in Ursa Major, what would be seen as quite significant about "Rockets in Ursa Major" is that the authors do not take their customary swipes at government and politicians. Faced with an extraterrestrial threat, politicians coming to their senses may well be the subliminal message being given out by this mellower approach to government and bureaucracy.

In the scene where Dick Warboys takes the beautiful female alien Alcyon on a trip to Dunwich, he explains to her how the two world wars of the twentieth century drained Britain financially. Britain forged ahead of the rest of the world in technological development and sold this technology to other nations. For this reason, Warboys felt confident that the Yela could be beaten and that the world would look to Britain for the technology whereby this could be accomplished. This part of the story no doubt emanates from the wartime experience of Fred Hoyle and his patriotic confidence in the future of Britain as a great nation.

Not only is this novel out of print but it has been removed from the stock of many public libraries. This is a great pity as so much can be gleaned from this story; as in so many of their other novels, many of the authors' predictions have still to come to pass. The book is by no means dated.

X

Seven Steps to the Sun:

by Fred Hoyle & Geoffrey Hoyle

In some of his writings, Fred Hoyle claimed that there was nothing particularly special about our own particular time period. If time could be compared to office pigeon holes in the dark and each pigeon hole represented a time period, and if each "time period" (pigeon-hole) were randomly illuminated, then one could travel backwards and forwards in time without even being aware of it. "Seven Steps to the Sun" (co-authored with Geoffrey Hoyle) is an amusing novel which goes quite a long way in capturing something of the concept of time - at least linearly advancing time - being illusory.

Mike Jerome, author, and central character in the novel is trying hard to come up with an idea for a TV script. A beautiful female masseur puts him in touch with a certain Professor Smitt. Jerome and Smitt discuss the idea of constructing a TV series based upon time travel. After leaving the Professor, Jerome, while crossing the street, is hit by a London cabby. On awakening in hospital he is discharged after being treated for carbon monoxide poisoning. He is somewhat astonished at this considering the nature of the accident which he had not long before experienced. Jerome soon finds that he has somehow traveled forward ten years in time and is now in quite a different world. This is the first of seven "time changes" which he goes through. After many thrilling adventures, Jerome finally wakens up in his own time period of 1969 and realises that it was all a dream, whose vividness was probably occasioned by the trauma of the accident. His best friend Pete Jones is there to greet him and all his familiar surroundings are restored. With the details of his dream fresh in his mind, Jerome gets to work on the plot of his story. Mike had seen Smitt in his dream but the other people with him had not. Now, back to awakened reality, he attempts to track down Smitt, but to no avail. No university in Britain claims to have a Professor Smitt on their staff. At the end of the novel, Jerome gets into a taxi and finds it is Professor Smitt who is at the wheel.

The reader of this novel could well be forgiven for being "left in mid-air" at this seemingly inconclusive ending. Was it all a dream? Or, was there an element of reality in what Jerome had experienced? Who is this "Professor Smitt?" What exactly is his game? Without there being a sequel to this novel, perhaps the authors are challenging their readers to figure out all of this for themselves. It is a real teaser and certainly gets the brain cells working overtime!

XI

The Molecule Men:

by Fred Hoyle & Geoffrey Hoyle

The Molecule Men" by Fred Hoyle and Mr. Geoffrey Hoyle is a most entertaining read. The main characteristic of the novels written by the Hoyles is that their science fiction generally has tremendous credibility in that they display clear linkages to science fact. However, when we see the villain of the piece, R. A. Adcock turn into a swarm of bees, then, at other parts in the story, into a white Pyrenean dog and afterwards, a white elephant, the reader could well be forgiven for a reaction which entailed the utterance "aw come on!" This expression of disbelief is soon abated when the main character in the story, Dr. John West, explains to Inspector Harrison that chemically a human being can be represented by a bag of coal, half a dozen cylinders of liquid air, a sack full of garden soil and a tank of water. Nature makes the oxygen, nitrogen, carbon and various other minerals into a human being by arranging these elements in the appropriate order. The plan for all living creatures is the genetic code. The materials remain the same, only they are used and arranged in different ways. Adcock represents a creature which has the ability to change its set of genetic instructions and so transform itself into any living creature. After this explanation, we soon ditch our initial "aw come on".

The Hoyles never fail to take a swipe at government and officialdom in their novels, and in this regard, "The Molecule Men" is no exception. The white elephant stomping around London and making its way to Westminster is an obvious metaphor representing the Hoyles' attitude towards the political establishment.

John West eventually discovers that the extraterrestrials have invaded the minds and bodies of the world's main political leaders - the British Prime Minister, The President of the USSR, the President of the USA and Chairman Mau. West explained to Adcock that he and his cohorts' fastening of themselves on to a few key political leaders would not give them the power which they so desired as the real decisions and real momentum for change came much further down the rungs of society. It was this explanation that eventually proved to be John West's undoing for when Adcock realised that West represented the level at which real power lay, West was singled out for invasion and would himself become a molecule man.

When we look at the four political leaders' strange and bizarre behaviour caused by Adcock's invasion of their minds, and then compare this with the conduct of present day politicians, we can be forgiven for wondering if there are not many R. A. Adcocks wandering around the world today!

There are in fact two novels contained in the book's overall title "The Molecule Men". The second one is entitled "The Monster of Loch Ness". In this story, the authors give us a taste of true Scottish culture as they write about such things as freak weather conditions, a ceilidh and a kelpie. The main character, Tom Cochrane is a retired Edinburgh University geography lecturer. Through Cochrane, the Hoyles articulate their displeasure at the way the education industry has developed since the 1960s. They talk about long-haired bedraggled students who have no individuality and who have no real interest in the subjects they are studying, their main reason for undertaking degree courses being merely to obtain the inevitable "piece of paper" in order to increase their chances of gaining employment. In his book "Man in the Universe" (1966) Fred Hoyle referred to this as "meal ticket" education.

The most surprising thing about this story is that the Hoyles have a completely different take on what the legendary Loch Ness Monster actually is. No doubt most readers' anticipation of the Loch Ness phenomenon is of some gigantic, pre-historic, dinosaur type creature emerging terrifyingly from the depths of Loch Ness and frightening the wits out of all and sundry in its vicinity. However, the Hoyles present the mystery of Loch Ness as a form of extraterrestrial life which wanted the loch's waters to re-charge itself.

The extraterrestrial dimension to the Loch Ness Monster may, like the molecule men, seem somewhat fantastical until we consider the traditional idea of "Nessie" from the point of view of the biological constraints nature imposes on ecosystems. There would have to be many

"Nessies". Over the centuries there would be an exponential growth in the family of monsters inhabiting the loch. The resources of the loch's ecosystem would plainly and simply be insufficient to sustain creatures of such physical proportions. Although the mystery surrounding Loch Ness is unlikely to be connected to extraterrestrial activity, an explanation of the Loch Ness phenomenon will have to be sought in areas which exclude the traditional idea of exotic pre-historic monsters.

XII

The Inferno:

by Fred Hoyle & Geoffrey Hoyle

Could the centre of our galaxy actually explode? Sounds too bizarre to be true? Then just read "The Inferno" by Fred and Geoffrey Hoyle and prepare yourself for a shock, for this book, like so many of the Hoyles' other science fiction works, contains convincing evidence of how science fiction is so closely related to science fact. Some galaxies do actually explode. Generally, these are known as Seyfert Galaxies. Considering how the stars in the central regions of our galaxy are, relatively speaking, densely packed together, we can surely see no reason why such an explosion could not in fact be triggered.

The story's main character, Cameron, who is a CERN physicist, discovers that the entire centre of our galaxy has indeed exploded. He warns the British government of the devastating consequences for the Earth when the radiation from the explosion reaches the outer arms of the galaxy. When the deadly radiation eventually strikes, there is a total breakdown of law and order and civil government. Cameron, who lives in the Highlands of Scotland, becomes a kind of Highland chieftain and organises law and civil government in an area extending from Kintail to Kyle. Thus, chapters 9, 10 and 11 of the novel can reasonably be considered as being a detailed modus operandi necessary in the event of the occurrence of a natural catastrophe of, quite literally, astronomical proportions!

"The Inferno" has woven into it many other interesting issues. The first third of the novel gives the layman a unique insight into the "office politics" of astronomy. What structural form should a new radiotelescope in Australia take? Astronomers argue over such issues as viewing time quotas and rotas. Little wonder then that the authors have Cameron describing astronomers as a "quarrelsome lot, notoriously". For anyone who is familiar with the Hoyles' novels, it will be of no surprise to the reader to find in "The Inferno", the contempt that Hoyle senior had for government – Cameron, at one point having had enough of the "drivel" spoken by those "who in fact know little or nothing". Another interesting aspect of this novel is the historical battle of Culloden and the social restructuring of the Highlands which ensued from the aftermath of this tragedy. If any phoenix has arisen from the ashes of the devastating radiation shower from the galactic centre, it is the restoration of a political system somewhat akin to the old Highland order. A righting of historical wrongs occurs but effected by means of a modern day catastrophe.

After some days of total darkness, the Earth's temperature and ecosystem start to recover and to display once again a semblance of normality. What caused this darkness and how the devastating crisis ended, Cameron could not fathom. It seemed to him that some force, some power, some superior cosmic intellect had intervened in a way which had over-ridden the laws of physics. Here, we descry an ending which differs so much from the usual conclusions of the Hoyles' novels. Perhaps it is reflective of Fred Hoyle's discovery of the fining-tuning aspects in the resonance properties of the carbon atom which brought him to the conclusion that an Intelligence of some form or another lay behind the Universe.

XIII

Into Deepest Space:

by Fred Hoyle & Geoffrey Hoyle

Like so many of Fred and Geoffrey Hoyle's novels, it is often difficult to tell if we are reading science fiction or science fact. "Into Deepest Space" is one of these stories where there would seem to be a great deal of overlap between fact and fiction. The Hoyles have written this novel in such a way that any reader could be completely forgiven for thinking that they are reading a technical treatise on how to accomplish not only inter-stellar space travel but inter-galactic travel as well. While reading through "Into Deepest Space", we enter into a process whereby we become incrementally convinced that inter-stellar and inter-galactic space travel are perfectly feasible propositions and that what must be lacking is the will and the financial wherewithal to do it. What appears not to be lacking though, is the actual practicality of deep space journeying even to the furthest reaches of the Universe.

"Into Deepest Space" is a sequel to "Rockets in Ursa Major". We see the same main cast of characters who decide to pursue the evil Yela and eliminate their threat to the galaxy. Dr. Richard Warboys and his three friends, Betelgeuse, Rigel and Alcyone, whose race have for centuries wandered the galaxy after their planet was destroyed by the Yela, have their huge space-ship taken in tow by the Yela. Unable to break free from the grip of the Yela craft, the four heroes are taken on a fifteen year journey to a quasar. Instead of being reduced to atoms when their craft enters the quasar, they survive to find themselves back in the solar system. When they reach Earth however, they discover that, due to the forces of relativity, a hundred million years of time have elapsed and the planet has reverted to a primitive form of barbarism.

When Warboys discovers that the living material on the planet is dextro-rotatory as opposed to levo-rotatory, his suspicions that they have entered an inverse Universe are confirmed. Do we live in a Universe of Black Hole/White Hole symmetry? The final part of the story will provoke much thought on this fundamental philosophical question. The other great philosophical matter brought up in this novel is about whether mankind can survive beyond a certain level of technological achievement. When the Earth's resources can no longer sustain the demands which exponential population growth places upon them, will the inevitable decline and eventual doom ensue? The authors suggested that we would not get beyond the year 2000. Here we are in 2015(at the time of writing) and humanity does not seem to be on the verge of extinction. Yet the Hoyles may only have been out in their timing, not in terms of the fundamental principle of the ultimate demise of the human species. As suggested in their book, humanity is a universal rather than a merely terrestrial phenomenon, and its expiration on one planet would not spell the termination of the species in galactic or inter-galactic dimensions. If however, we wish to save planet Earth's humanity, then perhaps we must transform into a practical and functioning reality, the kind of space travel envisioned by the authors in "Into Deepest Space" and, thus go into deepest space.

XIV

The Incandescent Ones:

by Fred Hoyle & Geoffrey Hoyle

Peter, an American student of Byzantine art at Moscow University, becomes embroiled in a tangled web of East/West intrigue after he receives a coded message from one of his professors during a lecture. As the plot thickens and unfolds, Peter soon discovers that what he has got himself landed in is of incredibly greater complexity and unbelievably more far-reaching than the relatively mundane on-going politico/diplomatic game of chess between the Soviets and the West.

What exactly is the mysterious "battery" that Peter has to smuggle across the Turkish-Soviet border? It is a contraption of great and profound mystery. Not only is it linked to the power sources that supply the Earth from an unknown source in space, but to the very nature of Peter and his "father" and to who and what they are.

"The Incandescent Ones" is another of Fred and Geoffrey Hoyle's novels where the seemingly impossible becomes possible. However, "The Incandescent Ones" goes that step further and brings even the ridiculously absurd within the confines of perfect credibility. The central character, the art student Peter, is a professional skier who can expertly negotiate his way over the most difficult of snow and ice terrains. But what about skiing over the gas clouds of the atmosphere of the giant planet Jupiter?!! Before one pulls grimaces with the inevitable accompanying "aw come on now", or "now the Hoyles have just taken it a bit too far this time", one should carefully read the technical and scientific explanation rendered by the authors through one of their characters, Edelstam, on how this stupendous feat can actually be accomplished. The reader, when having finished digesting the technical instructions on how to perform this phenomenal act, will surely come away nodding his head and saying, "yes, one day people will skim over the Jovian atmosphere on skis!" A word of warning for the reader though: the book is anything but easy to put down.

XV

The Westminster Disaster:
by Fred Hoyle & Geoffrey Hoyle

"The Westminster Disaster" is a thriller of a novel written by Fred and Geoffrey Hoyle. The opening chapter is entitled "The Threads", and there are very many threads in this story; different issues, different people in a variety of places, different political perspectives and conflicting interests. Yet, like contributories, these diverse strands all connect in one fast flowing river. Thus, it is a story that demands that the reader keep his wits about him, for failing to do so, he can quite easily lose one or two of the threads. However, for the vigilant and persevering mind, reading through "The Westminster Disaster" will bring about great rewards – firstly in being treated to a riveting story, and secondly in discovering the subtlety and versatility of the minds which composed the epic.

So, what do we have in the novel? It all begins with the Canadian company, International Heavy Metals, which aspires to buy into uranium mining operations in South Africa and transfer to that country some state-of-the-art technology. However, the South Africa of the 1970's was a very hot political potato. The Soviets, with a desire to stop the deal, plan a motion for sanctions against South Africa in the Security Council of the United Nations. To counter this, the Americans aim to get the British to veto the motion in exchange for American assistance with the debts piled up by Britain during the 1970's.

And how desperate are the Soviets to prevent a British veto at the UN? Desperate enough to organise a band of international terrorists to smuggle uranium to Britain for the purpose of manufacturing a bomb capable of destroying London. Igor Markov, the KGB mastermind behind the operation, had planned that the five accomplices who were to make and plant the device in London were initially unknown to each other.

What happens though, when each of them starts to see things from a different perspective and so start to devise their own conflicting agendas? This is when it all really gets exciting!

There are some rather explicit sex scenes in the book when one of the terrorists, Anna Morgue, forces her compatriot, Hermann Kapp, at gunpoint, to have intercourse with her. That the sex scenes occur after Morgue has committed a murder, clearly shows the sort of ghastly psychology that turns her on! If any reviewer were to write something to the effect of "don't let your children in their formative years read this book", there would be an immediate interest shown in it by adults, and a desire for the younger ones to get a hold of it once they have emerged from tender age!

XVI

The Energy Pirate:

by Fred Hoyle & Geoffrey Hoyle

"The Energy Pirate" by Fred and Geoffrey Hoyle is a short Ladybird children's science fiction story. Like another story in the series (The Giants of Universal Park), "The Energy Pirate" features the mysterious Professor Gamma, his daughter Kiryl and her friend William.

The story centresaround the theft of Earth's sugar by Professor Gamma's old friend named Zuchario. William is deprived of his weekly Neutron Chocolate Bar due to the theft of the sugar, and so he, along with Professor Gamma and Kiryl set out to find what is at the bottom of these bizarre goings-on.

Even in this short little Ladybird Book story, something of the science fact can be gleaned if one looks and thinks hard enough. Professor Gamma's pipe has the astonishing ability to dematerialise people and transport them through the energy pathways of the Universe. This is somewhat reminiscent of "worms" which many scientists believe may exist in the Universe and which have time and space bending properties thus enabling travel through the cosmos in literally no time at all! Zuchario's insatiable need for sugar as a source of power brings to mind the ongoing need to search for an alternative to fossil fuel.

At the end of the story, the three heroes succeed in putting an end to Zuchario's escapade, and so, the Earth's sugar - and thus its life - is saved from annihilation. On top of all of this, William gets his Neutron Chocolate Bar, which he discovers has the unbelievable quality of renewing itself. In future, it may not be beyond the means of science to find ways of getting the right atoms in the right combination at the right time and place so that children may be presented with what must be their ultimate dream - a re-chargeable chocolate bar!

XVII

The Frozen Planet of Azuron:

by Fred & Geoffrey Hoyle

Even in a little Ladybird children's story such as this, a lot of science fact can be gleaned – such is the genius of Fred and Geoffrey Hoyle. William, Professor Gamma and his daughter Kiryl set out along the energy pathways of the Universe to catch Absolute Zero, the fiend who has found a way to convert heat into action. Zero has been sucking up heat everywhere he goes in the Universe and using it for no good purpose. Perhaps one dayscientists will find a way to convert heat into action.

The story is full of strange creatures and strange phenomena: a transparent dog which looks like it is made of crystal; ghost like entities that appear out of nowhere and an entire universe in a carrier bag.

Fred Hoyle often averred that the range of the Universe which our telescopes permit us to observe does not represent the cosmos in its entirety. More recently, Professor Paul Davies has referred to "cosmic regions" wherein may operate completely different laws of physics. Where different laws of physics exist, there will be different laws of biology, so "The Frozen Planet of Azuron" may well be nearer to reality than even its authors imagined.

Another view

"The Frozen Planet of Azuron is a well illustrated 51 page Ladybird book written by Fred Hoyle and Geoffrey Hoyle for the enjoyment of young children. Professor Gamma, with his daughter Kiryl and their friend William, constitute the main caste of characters who set out on a quest to catch the villain who is causing ice ages to occur, not only on the Earth, but on great numbers of planets throughout the Universe.

While many of the incidents depicted in the story, such as the professor's pipe which can transport himself and his friends along the energy pathways of the Universe, a metal box that gives out carbon soot particles, a transparent dog that melts into a pool of water, and another transparent dog the size of a man that transmogrifies into the villain, Absolute Zero, one who knows Fred Hoyle the scientist as well as Fred Hoyle the novelist, will be able to discern much of Hoyle's mindset in this little work of fiction.

The unusually cold weather which is at the centre of this story has overtones of the climatological disaster which could overtake the Earth should it be struck by a large enough meteorite. By highlighting in his book, "Ice: The Ultimate Human Catastrophe" (Continuum International Publishing Group, Limited, 1981), the fact that in geological time spans, the Earth has been more vulnerable to ice ages rather than to the extremes of heat, and that there is no reason to aver that this pattern will change in future geological eras, Hoyle presents a catastrophe quite at variance with the standard "global warming" hypothesis.

That the "energy pathways" of the Universe which allow Professor Gamma and his friends to reach far off planets in virtually no time at all are very similar to the idea of "worm-holes," and that Black-hole Space contained in a carpet-bag brings to mind the phenomenon of Black Holes and the strange world of Quantum Mechanics, are all indicative of the brilliant scientific mind of Fred Hoyle shining forth from these pages of fantasy.

Towards the end of the story, when the villain has been vanquished, the ice melts and life starts erupting forth throughout Azuron, the Hoyle aficionado will easily discern here, the connection with Hoyle's works in which he examines evolutionary stages in relation to the ending of ice ages ("Diseases from Space," Harper & Row, 1980 [with N.C. Wickramasinghe]; "Ice: The Ultimate Human Catastrophe" Continuum International Publishing Group, Limited, 1981; "Evolution from Space" Flamingo; 1983 [with N.C. Wickramasinghe].

All in all, whether one is a "serious scientist," or just a sci fi enthusiast, this little Ladybird book is a worthwhile read for relaxation and enjoyment.

XVIII

The Giants of Universal Park:

by Fred and Geoffrey Hoyle

Though a fun book in the Ladybird series, "The Giants of Universal Park" shows the great versatility of Fred Hoyle and Geoffrey Hoyle. Yet even in a short story which contains more magic than it does science, we can still, if we peer through the fantasia carefully enough, discern many connections to serious science.

Professor Gamma, with his daughter Kiryl and their friend, William, travel through the "energy pathways of the Universe" to a distant planet. These "energy pathways" could well have connotations to the wormholes theorised by astrophysicists and considered by both science fiction and science fact writers as ways of overcoming the vast distances in the Universe.

While the theft of the Earth's sun by galactic star thieves may be a bit too incredible for most readers, nevertheless, it could well be seen as an indication of the future commercialisation of space.

In the bizarre match between the Giants and the Magnetics, the "football" was a beam of light which was deflected by the Magnetics by their making of themselves into black holes, whereas the Giants kicked it "….by using the scattering of light by light". The properties of black holes and their affect upon light are clearly alluded to here.

All in all, the book is a fun and relaxing read for both adults and children alike with the discerning reader being able to tease out from the bizarre events it depicts, some very interesting scientific concepts which are still the subject of investigation and research by scientists 33 years after the story was composed.

XIX

The Planet of Death:

by Fred & Geoffrey Hoyle

It is surely the genius of Fred Hoyle and his son Geoffrey that a small fun Ladybird book of a mere fifty one pages can be packed with so much credible science. As in the other Ladybird books written by the Hoyles, The Planet of Death depicts the same heroic dramatis personae – Professor Gamma and his daughter Kiryl with their friend William – gallivanting around the Universe in their brave effort to save the Earth from one or other of its deadly foes. And just how do our heroes charge around the vast distances of inter-galactic space? By the bending of space and time inside the Universe's energy routes which theoretical physicists now term 'worm-holes.' The contortions to which Professor Gamma and our other two heroes are subjected to when travelling along these energy pathways closely mimic what would happen to anyone who encountered the misfortune of falling into a black hole, where gravity is so strong that not even light can escape from its eerie dark clutches.

When considering the plot of the story and the villain of the piece, Viro, who is spreading viruses and bacteria around the Universe - and in this instance, the French Ague to the Earth - anyone familiar with the works of Fred Hoyle and his colleague, Professor N. Chandra Wickramasinghe, will not fail to descry in this short tale a subtle hint of Hoyle's and Wickramasinghe's research on various cold and influenza pandemics which has led them in the unconventional direction of contending that pathogenic material has its origins in interstellar gas clouds and is brought to planets principally by cometary and asteroidal mechanistic functions. While it has been to the bafflement of conventional epidemiology in attempting to explain the sudden appearance and disappearance of a number of viral types, Hoyle's and

Wickramasinghe's offer of a solution to this mystery by bringing space incident pathogens into the equation is mirrored in the last page of the book where the doctor attending upon William exclaims "Nobody has had the Red Flu in twenty years, we can't think where he got it from," but which William in the picture, lying in bed, thermometer in his mouth and pointing at a red scar on his forearm, winks a mischievous 'but I know' cheekily at the reader!

XX

Comet Halley:

by Fred Hoyle

Contrary to generally accepted wisdom, Fred Hoyle once claimed that a person is not always at their most creative and productive during their years of so-called youthful vigour. "Comet Halley" bears great testimony to this statement as it was Hoyle's last novel and by far his best. Published in the last 16 years of the author's life, this book contains over 400 pages of thrills and excitement. Hoyle's fictional writings are always peppered with a very generous sprinkling of sound science which so tends to leave the reader with the feeling that "this could be true – it is not entirely impossible". This story would make even the hardest sceptic consider, if even for just a brief moment, that comets may well contain some sort of living and intelligent entity. For those who know a little bit of astronomy and thus realise that it is still a mystery as to what exactly the propulsion mechanism is that drives comets on their highly elliptical orbit around the solar system or even where comets originate, the feeling that comets may be conscious entities will be rendered added impetus. However, "Comet Halley" is more than science fiction; it contains a murder mystery of Agatha Christie proportions, the "office politics" of universities and research establishments, the real politics of the nation, a supernatural element with ghostly goings on and a love story involving the two central characters in the plot (Professor Isaac Newton and Frances Margaret Haroldson). All these elements being rolled into one and given the added excitement of being placed within the Cold War context and superpower rivalry, but with a third superpower coming into play – Halley's Comet itself - is what makes this novel nothing less than an absolute masterpiece of literary composition. "Comet Halley" is better appreciated by the reader who is in possession of a background knowledge of Fred Hoyle's theories regarding panspermia origins of life and the cosmic origin of many diseases – most notably influenza outbreaks. These theories, developed by Hoyle and his colleague, Professor N. Chandra Wickramasinghe, postulate that life is not a localised terrestrial phenomenon, but is rather, something which is built into the very fabric of the Universe in the form of bacteria and virii which form in interstellar gas clouds and are transported to solid bodies like planets by means of comets. "Comet Halley", Hoyle's last novel (1985) mirrors his first novel, "The Black Cloud" (1959) in that it involves the notion of life evolving on a body other than a planet or a moon. While the Cloud in the first novel brings death and destruction, the Comet in the final novel is a harbinger of peace and goodwill in that it shows the futility of weapons of mass destruction and superpower confrontation. Finally, the Comet fires off something like a missile which hits the North Pole with great accuracy and explosive force yet without killing a single soul. This impact causes the polar ice caps to start melting. However, it is a global warming of a positive kind for it will soon extend the agricultural potential of the globe by bringing into production hitherto unviable farming areas such as northern Canada and Siberia. This ties in with Hoyle's contention that the vehicle for global disaster will be another ice age and not what we call "global warming". A large sized asteroid or meteorite hitting the Earth in a place where reflective dust particles would be flung up into the atmosphere where they would blot out sunlight, would immediately bring about the next ice age. "Comet Halley" offers an alternative model for the future of humanity both in terms of science and politics.

Printed in the United States
By Bookmasters